C-2672   CAREER EXAMINATION SERIES

This is your
PASSBOOK for...

Graphic Arts Specialist

Test Preparation Study Guide
Questions & Answers

COPYRIGHT NOTICE

This book is SOLELY intended for, is sold ONLY to, and its use is RESTRICTED to individual, bona fide applicants or candidates who qualify by virtue of having seriously filed applications for appropriate license, certificate, professional and/or promotional advancement, higher school matriculation, scholarship, or other legitimate requirements of education and/or governmental authorities.

This book is NOT intended for use, class instruction, tutoring, training, duplication, copying, reprinting, excerption, or adaptation, etc., by:

1) Other publishers
2) Proprietors and/or Instructors of "Coaching" and/or Preparatory Courses
3) Personnel and/or Training Divisions of commercial, industrial, and governmental organizations
4) Schools, colleges, or universities and/or their departments and staffs, including teachers and other personnel
5) Testing Agencies or Bureaus
6) Study groups which seek by the purchase of a single volume to copy and/or duplicate and/or adapt this material for use by the group as a whole without having purchased individual volumes for each of the members of the group
7) Et al.

Such persons would be in violation of appropriate Federal and State statutes.

PROVISION OF LICENSING AGREEMENTS – Recognized educational, commercial, industrial, and governmental institutions and organizations, and others legitimately engaged in educational pursuits, including training, testing, and measurement activities, may address request for a licensing agreement to the copyright owners, who will determine whether, and under what conditions, including fees and charges, the materials in this book may be used them. In other words, a licensing facility exists for the legitimate use of the material in this book on other than an individual basis. However, it is asseverated and affirmed here that the material in this book CANNOT be used without the receipt of the express permission of such a licensing agreement from the Publishers. Inquiries re licensing should be addressed to the company, attention rights and permissions department.

All rights reserved, including the right of reproduction in whole or in part, in any form or by any means, electronic or mechanical, including photocopying, recording, or by any information storage and retrieval system, without permission in writing from the Publisher.

Copyright © 2025 by
National Learning Corporation

212 Michael Drive, Syosset, NY 11791
(516) 921-8888 • www.passbooks.com
E-mail: info@passbooks.com

PASSBOOK® SERIES

THE *PASSBOOK® SERIES* has been created to prepare applicants and candidates for the ultimate academic battlefield – the examination room.

At some time in our lives, each and every one of us may be required to take an examination – for validation, matriculation, admission, qualification, registration, certification, or licensure.

Based on the assumption that every applicant or candidate has met the basic formal educational standards, has taken the required number of courses, and read the necessary texts, the *PASSBOOK® SERIES* furnishes the one special preparation which may assure passing with confidence, instead of failing with insecurity. Examination questions – together with answers – are furnished as the basic vehicle for study so that the mysteries of the examination and its compounding difficulties may be eliminated or diminished by a sure method.

This book is meant to help you pass your examination provided that you qualify and are serious in your objective.

The entire field is reviewed through the huge store of content information which is succinctly presented through a provocative and challenging approach – the question-and-answer method.

A climate of success is established by furnishing the correct answers at the end of each test.

You soon learn to recognize types of questions, forms of questions, and patterns of questioning. You may even begin to anticipate expected outcomes.

You perceive that many questions are repeated or adapted so that you can gain acute insights, which may enable you to score many sure points.

You learn how to confront new questions, or types of questions, and to attack them confidently and work out the correct answers.

You note objectives and emphases, and recognize pitfalls and dangers, so that you may make positive educational adjustments.

Moreover, you are kept fully informed in relation to new concepts, methods, practices, and directions in the field.

You discover that you are actually taking the examination all the time: you are preparing for the examination by "taking" an examination, not by reading extraneous and/or supererogatory textbooks.

In short, this PASSBOOK®, used directedly, should be an important factor in helping you to pass your test.

GRAPHIC ARTS SPECIALIST

DUTIES
Conceives, roughs out, and produces graphic and other art work for signs, posters, exhibits, publications, etc., utilizing a wide variety of art equipment and media. Performs related duties as required.

SUBJECT OF EXAMINATION
The written test is designed to test knowledges, skills, and/or labilities in such areas as:
1. Knowledge of commonly used commercial art and drafting equipment, materials, and supplies;
2. Principles of copy and art preparation;
3. Basic knowledge of major commercial printing and reproduction processes, materials, and equipment;
4. Knowledge of contemporary methods of preparing layouts and mechanicals; and

HOW TO TAKE A TEST

I. YOU MUST PASS AN EXAMINATION

A. *WHAT EVERY CANDIDATE SHOULD KNOW*

Examination applicants often ask us for help in preparing for the written test. What can I study in advance? What kinds of questions will be asked? How will the test be given? How will the papers be graded?

As an applicant for a civil service examination, you may be wondering about some of these things. Our purpose here is to suggest effective methods of advance study and to describe civil service examinations.

Your chances for success on this examination can be increased if you know how to prepare. Those "pre-examination jitters" can be reduced if you know what to expect. You can even experience an adventure in good citizenship if you know why civil service exams are given.

B. *WHY ARE CIVIL SERVICE EXAMINATIONS GIVEN?*

Civil service examinations are important to you in two ways. As a citizen, you want public jobs filled by employees who know how to do their work. As a job seeker, you want a fair chance to compete for that job on an equal footing with other candidates. The best-known means of accomplishing this two-fold goal is the competitive examination.

Exams are widely publicized throughout the nation. They may be administered for jobs in federal, state, city, municipal, town or village governments or agencies.

Any citizen may apply, with some limitations, such as the age or residence of applicants. Your experience and education may be reviewed to see whether you meet the requirements for the particular examination. When these requirements exist, they are reasonable and applied consistently to all applicants. Thus, a competitive examination may cause you some uneasiness now, but it is your privilege and safeguard.

C. *HOW ARE CIVIL SERVICE EXAMS DEVELOPED?*

Examinations are carefully written by trained technicians who are specialists in the field known as "psychological measurement," in consultation with recognized authorities in the field of work that the test will cover. These experts recommend the subject matter areas or skills to be tested; only those knowledges or skills important to your success on the job are included. The most reliable books and source materials available are used as references. Together, the experts and technicians judge the difficulty level of the questions.

Test technicians know how to phrase questions so that the problem is clearly stated. Their ethics do not permit "trick" or "catch" questions. Questions may have been tried out on sample groups, or subjected to statistical analysis, to determine their usefulness.

Written tests are often used in combination with performance tests, ratings of training and experience, and oral interviews. All of these measures combine to form the best-known means of finding the right person for the right job.

II. HOW TO PASS THE WRITTEN TEST

A. NATURE OF THE EXAMINATION

To prepare intelligently for civil service examinations, you should know how they differ from school examinations you have taken. In school you were assigned certain definite pages to read or subjects to cover. The examination questions were quite detailed and usually emphasized memory. Civil service exams, on the other hand, try to discover your present ability to perform the duties of a position, plus your potentiality to learn these duties. In other words, a civil service exam attempts to predict how successful you will be. Questions cover such a broad area that they cannot be as minute and detailed as school exam questions.

In the public service similar kinds of work, or positions, are grouped together in one "class." This process is known as *position-classification*. All the positions in a class are paid according to the salary range for that class. One class title covers all of these positions, and they are all tested by the same examination.

B. FOUR BASIC STEPS

1) Study the announcement

How, then, can you know what subjects to study? Our best answer is: "Learn as much as possible about the class of positions for which you've applied." The exam will test the knowledge, skills and abilities needed to do the work.

Your most valuable source of information about the position you want is the official exam announcement. This announcement lists the training and experience qualifications. Check these standards and apply only if you come reasonably close to meeting them.

The brief description of the position in the examination announcement offers some clues to the subjects which will be tested. Think about the job itself. Review the duties in your mind. Can you perform them, or are there some in which you are rusty? Fill in the blank spots in your preparation.

Many jurisdictions preview the written test in the exam announcement by including a section called "Knowledge and Abilities Required," "Scope of the Examination," or some similar heading. Here you will find out specifically what fields will be tested.

2) Review your own background

Once you learn in general what the position is all about, and what you need to know to do the work, ask yourself which subjects you already know fairly well and which need improvement. You may wonder whether to concentrate on improving your strong areas or on building some background in your fields of weakness. When the announcement has specified "some knowledge" or "considerable knowledge," or has used adjectives like "beginning principles of…" or "advanced … methods," you can get a clue as to the number and difficulty of questions to be asked in any given field. More questions, and hence broader coverage, would be included for those subjects which are more important in the work. Now weigh your strengths and weaknesses against the job requirements and prepare accordingly.

3) Determine the level of the position

Another way to tell how intensively you should prepare is to understand the level of the job for which you are applying. Is it the entering level? In other words, is this the position in which beginners in a field of work are hired? Or is it an intermediate or advanced level? Sometimes this is indicated by such words as "Junior" or "Senior" in the class title. Other jurisdictions use Roman numerals to designate the level – Clerk I, Clerk II, for example. The word "Supervisor" sometimes appears in the title. If the level is not indicated by the title, check the description of duties. Will you be working under very close supervision, or will you have responsibility for independent decisions in this work?

4) Choose appropriate study materials

Now that you know the subjects to be examined and the relative amount of each subject to be covered, you can choose suitable study materials. For beginning level jobs, or even advanced ones, if you have a pronounced weakness in some aspect of your training, read a modern, standard textbook in that field. Be sure it is up to date and has general coverage. Such books are normally available at your library, and the librarian will be glad to help you locate one. For entry-level positions, questions of appropriate difficulty are chosen – neither highly advanced questions, nor those too simple. Such questions require careful thought but not advanced training.

If the position for which you are applying is technical or advanced, you will read more advanced, specialized material. If you are already familiar with the basic principles of your field, elementary textbooks would waste your time. Concentrate on advanced textbooks and technical periodicals. Think through the concepts and review difficult problems in your field.

These are all general sources. You can get more ideas on your own initiative, following these leads. For example, training manuals and publications of the government agency which employs workers in your field can be useful, particularly for technical and professional positions. A letter or visit to the government department involved may result in more specific study suggestions, and certainly will provide you with a more definite idea of the exact nature of the position you are seeking.

III. KINDS OF TESTS

Tests are used for purposes other than measuring knowledge and ability to perform specified duties. For some positions, it is equally important to test ability to make adjustments to new situations or to profit from training. In others, basic mental abilities not dependent on information are essential. Questions which test these things may not appear as pertinent to the duties of the position as those which test for knowledge and information. Yet they are often highly important parts of a fair examination. For very general questions, it is almost impossible to help you direct your study efforts. What we can do is to point out some of the more common of these general abilities needed in public service positions and describe some typical questions.

1) General information

Broad, general information has been found useful for predicting job success in some kinds of work. This is tested in a variety of ways, from vocabulary lists to questions about current events. Basic background in some field of work, such as sociology or economics, may be sampled in a group of questions. Often these are principles which have become familiar to most persons through exposure rather than through formal training. It is difficult to advise you how to study for these questions; being alert to the world around you is our best suggestion.

2) Verbal ability

An example of an ability needed in many positions is verbal or language ability. Verbal ability is, in brief, the ability to use and understand words. Vocabulary and grammar tests are typical measures of this ability. Reading comprehension or paragraph interpretation questions are common in many kinds of civil service tests. You are given a paragraph of written material and asked to find its central meaning.

3) Numerical ability

Number skills can be tested by the familiar arithmetic problem, by checking paired lists of numbers to see which are alike and which are different, or by interpreting charts and graphs. In the latter test, a graph may be printed in the test booklet which you are asked to use as the basis for answering questions.

4) Observation

A popular test for law-enforcement positions is the observation test. A picture is shown to you for several minutes, then taken away. Questions about the picture test your ability to observe both details and larger elements.

5) Following directions

In many positions in the public service, the employee must be able to carry out written instructions dependably and accurately. You may be given a chart with several columns, each column listing a variety of information. The questions require you to carry out directions involving the information given in the chart.

6) Skills and aptitudes

Performance tests effectively measure some manual skills and aptitudes. When the skill is one in which you are trained, such as typing or shorthand, you can practice. These tests are often very much like those given in business school or high school courses. For many of the other skills and aptitudes, however, no short-time preparation can be made. Skills and abilities natural to you or that you have developed throughout your lifetime are being tested.

Many of the general questions just described provide all the data needed to answer the questions and ask you to use your reasoning ability to find the answers. Your best preparation for these tests, as well as for tests of facts and ideas, is to be at your physical and mental best. You, no doubt, have your own methods of getting into an exam-taking mood and keeping "in shape." The next section lists some ideas on this subject.

IV. KINDS OF QUESTIONS

Only rarely is the "essay" question, which you answer in narrative form, used in civil service tests. Civil service tests are usually of the short-answer type. Full instructions for answering these questions will be given to you at the examination. But in case this is your first experience with short-answer questions and separate answer sheets, here is what you need to know:

1) Multiple-choice Questions

Most popular of the short-answer questions is the "multiple choice" or "best answer" question. It can be used, for example, to test for factual knowledge, ability to solve problems or judgment in meeting situations found at work.

A multiple-choice question is normally one of three types—
- It can begin with an incomplete statement followed by several possible endings. You are to find the one ending which *best* completes the statement, although some of the others may not be entirely wrong.
- It can also be a complete statement in the form of a question which is answered by choosing one of the statements listed.

- It can be in the form of a problem – again you select the best answer.

Here is an example of a multiple-choice question with a discussion which should give you some clues as to the method for choosing the right answer:

When an employee has a complaint about his assignment, the action which will *best* help him overcome his difficulty is to
- A. discuss his difficulty with his coworkers
- B. take the problem to the head of the organization
- C. take the problem to the person who gave him the assignment
- D. say nothing to anyone about his complaint

In answering this question, you should study each of the choices to find which is best. Consider choice "A" – Certainly an employee may discuss his complaint with fellow employees, but no change or improvement can result, and the complaint remains unresolved. Choice "B" is a poor choice since the head of the organization probably does not know what assignment you have been given, and taking your problem to him is known as "going over the head" of the supervisor. The supervisor, or person who made the assignment, is the person who can clarify it or correct any injustice. Choice "C" is, therefore, correct. To say nothing, as in choice "D," is unwise. Supervisors have and interest in knowing the problems employees are facing, and the employee is seeking a solution to his problem.

2) True/False Questions

The "true/false" or "right/wrong" form of question is sometimes used. Here a complete statement is given. Your job is to decide whether the statement is right or wrong.

SAMPLE: A roaming cell-phone call to a nearby city costs less than a non-roaming call to a distant city.

This statement is wrong, or false, since roaming calls are more expensive.

This is not a complete list of all possible question forms, although most of the others are variations of these common types. You will always get complete directions for answering questions. Be sure you understand *how* to mark your answers – ask questions until you do.

V. RECORDING YOUR ANSWERS

Computer terminals are used more and more today for many different kinds of exams.

For an examination with very few applicants, you may be told to record your answers in the test booklet itself. Separate answer sheets are much more common. If this separate answer sheet is to be scored by machine – and this is often the case – it is highly important that you mark your answers correctly in order to get credit.

An electronic scoring machine is often used in civil service offices because of the speed with which papers can be scored. Machine-scored answer sheets must be marked with a pencil, which will be given to you. This pencil has a high graphite content which responds to the electronic scoring machine. As a matter of fact, stray dots may register as answers, so do not let your pencil rest on the answer sheet while you are pondering the correct answer. Also, if your pencil lead breaks or is otherwise defective, ask for another.

Since the answer sheet will be dropped in a slot in the scoring machine, be careful not to bend the corners or get the paper crumpled.

The answer sheet normally has five vertical columns of numbers, with 30 numbers to a column. These numbers correspond to the question numbers in your test booklet. After each number, going across the page are four or five pairs of dotted lines. These short dotted lines have small letters or numbers above them. The first two pairs may also have a "T" or "F" above the letters. This indicates that the first two pairs only are to be used if the questions are of the true-false type. If the questions are multiple choice, disregard the "T" and "F" and pay attention only to the small letters or numbers.

Answer your questions in the manner of the sample that follows:

32. The largest city in the United States is
    A. Washington, D.C.
    B. New York City
    C. Chicago
    D. Detroit
    E. San Francisco

1) Choose the answer you think is best. (New York City is the largest, so "B" is correct.)
2) Find the row of dotted lines numbered the same as the question you are answering. (Find row number 32)
3) Find the pair of dotted lines corresponding to the answer. (Find the pair of lines under the mark "B.")
4) Make a solid black mark between the dotted lines.

VI. BEFORE THE TEST

Common sense will help you find procedures to follow to get ready for an examination. Too many of us, however, overlook these sensible measures. Indeed, nervousness and fatigue have been found to be the most serious reasons why applicants fail to do their best on civil service tests. Here is a list of reminders:

- Begin your preparation early – Don't wait until the last minute to go scurrying around for books and materials or to find out what the position is all about.
- Prepare continuously – An hour a night for a week is better than an all-night cram session. This has been definitely established. What is more, a night a week for a month will return better dividends than crowding your study into a shorter period of time.
- Locate the place of the exam – You have been sent a notice telling you when and where to report for the examination. If the location is in a different town or otherwise unfamiliar to you, it would be well to inquire the best route and learn something about the building.
- Relax the night before the test – Allow your mind to rest. Do not study at all that night. Plan some mild recreation or diversion; then go to bed early and get a good night's sleep.
- Get up early enough to make a leisurely trip to the place for the test – This way unforeseen events, traffic snarls, unfamiliar buildings, etc. will not upset you.
- Dress comfortably – A written test is not a fashion show. You will be known by number and not by name, so wear something comfortable.

- Leave excess paraphernalia at home – Shopping bags and odd bundles will get in your way. You need bring only the items mentioned in the official notice you received; usually everything you need is provided. Do not bring reference books to the exam. They will only confuse those last minutes and be taken away from you when in the test room.
- Arrive somewhat ahead of time – If because of transportation schedules you must get there very early, bring a newspaper or magazine to take your mind off yourself while waiting.
- Locate the examination room – When you have found the proper room, you will be directed to the seat or part of the room where you will sit. Sometimes you are given a sheet of instructions to read while you are waiting. Do not fill out any forms until you are told to do so; just read them and be prepared.
- Relax and prepare to listen to the instructions
- If you have any physical problem that may keep you from doing your best, be sure to tell the test administrator. If you are sick or in poor health, you really cannot do your best on the exam. You can come back and take the test some other time.

VII. AT THE TEST

The day of the test is here and you have the test booklet in your hand. The temptation to get going is very strong. Caution! There is more to success than knowing the right answers. You must know how to identify your papers and understand variations in the type of short-answer question used in this particular examination. Follow these suggestions for maximum results from your efforts:

1) Cooperate with the monitor

The test administrator has a duty to create a situation in which you can be as much at ease as possible. He will give instructions, tell you when to begin, check to see that you are marking your answer sheet correctly, and so on. He is not there to guard you, although he will see that your competitors do not take unfair advantage. He wants to help you do your best.

2) Listen to all instructions

Don't jump the gun! Wait until you understand all directions. In most civil service tests you get more time than you need to answer the questions. So don't be in a hurry. Read each word of instructions until you clearly understand the meaning. Study the examples, listen to all announcements and follow directions. Ask questions if you do not understand what to do.

3) Identify your papers

Civil service exams are usually identified by number only. You will be assigned a number; you must not put your name on your test papers. Be sure to copy your number correctly. Since more than one exam may be given, copy your exact examination title.

4) Plan your time

Unless you are told that a test is a "speed" or "rate of work" test, speed itself is usually not important. Time enough to answer all the questions will be provided, but this does not mean that you have all day. An overall time limit has been set. Divide the total time (in minutes) by the number of questions to determine the approximate time you have for each question.

5) Do not linger over difficult questions

If you come across a difficult question, mark it with a paper clip (useful to have along) and come back to it when you have been through the booklet. One caution if you do this – be sure to skip a number on your answer sheet as well. Check often to be sure that you have not lost your place and that you are marking in the row numbered the same as the question you are answering.

6) Read the questions

Be sure you know what the question asks! Many capable people are unsuccessful because they failed to *read* the questions correctly.

7) Answer all questions

Unless you have been instructed that a penalty will be deducted for incorrect answers, it is better to guess than to omit a question.

8) Speed tests

It is often better NOT to guess on speed tests. It has been found that on timed tests people are tempted to spend the last few seconds before time is called in marking answers at random – without even reading them – in the hope of picking up a few extra points. To discourage this practice, the instructions may warn you that your score will be "corrected" for guessing. That is, a penalty will be applied. The incorrect answers will be deducted from the correct ones, or some other penalty formula will be used.

9) Review your answers

If you finish before time is called, go back to the questions you guessed or omitted to give them further thought. Review other answers if you have time.

10) Return your test materials

If you are ready to leave before others have finished or time is called, take ALL your materials to the monitor and leave quietly. Never take any test material with you. The monitor can discover whose papers are not complete, and taking a test booklet may be grounds for disqualification.

VIII. EXAMINATION TECHNIQUES

1) Read the general instructions carefully. These are usually printed on the first page of the exam booklet. As a rule, these instructions refer to the timing of the examination; the fact that you should not start work until the signal and must stop work at a signal, etc. If there are any *special* instructions, such as a choice of questions to be answered, make sure that you note this instruction carefully.

2) When you are ready to start work on the examination, that is as soon as the signal has been given, read the instructions to each question booklet, underline any key words or phrases, such as *least, best, outline, describe* and the like. In this way you will tend to answer as requested rather than discover on reviewing your paper that you *listed without describing*, that you selected the *worst* choice rather than the *best* choice, etc.

3) If the examination is of the objective or multiple-choice type – that is, each question will also give a series of possible answers: A, B, C or D, and you are called upon to select the best answer and write the letter next to that answer on your answer paper – it is advisable to start answering each question in turn. There may be anywhere from 50 to 100 such questions in the three or four hours allotted and you can see how much time would be taken if you read through all the questions before beginning to answer any. Furthermore, if you come across a question or group of questions which you know would be difficult to answer, it would undoubtedly affect your handling of all the other questions.

4) If the examination is of the essay type and contains but a few questions, it is a moot point as to whether you should read all the questions before starting to answer any one. Of course, if you are given a choice – say five out of seven and the like – then it is essential to read all the questions so you can eliminate the two that are most difficult. If, however, you are asked to answer all the questions, there may be danger in trying to answer the easiest one first because you may find that you will spend too much time on it. The best technique is to answer the first question, then proceed to the second, etc.

5) Time your answers. Before the exam begins, write down the time it started, then add the time allowed for the examination and write down the time it must be completed, then divide the time available somewhat as follows:
   - If 3-1/2 hours are allowed, that would be 210 minutes. If you have 80 objective-type questions, that would be an average of 2-1/2 minutes per question. Allow yourself no more than 2 minutes per question, or a total of 160 minutes, which will permit about 50 minutes to review.
   - If for the time allotment of 210 minutes there are 7 essay questions to answer, that would average about 30 minutes a question. Give yourself only 25 minutes per question so that you have about 35 minutes to review.

6) The most important instruction is to *read each question* and make sure you know what is wanted. The second most important instruction is to *time yourself properly* so that you answer every question. The third most important instruction is to *answer every question*. Guess if you have to but include something for each question. Remember that you will receive no credit for a blank and will probably receive some credit if you write something in answer to an essay question. If you guess a letter – say "B" for a multiple-choice question – you may have guessed right. If you leave a blank as an answer to a multiple-choice question, the examiners may respect your feelings but it will not add a point to your score. Some exams may penalize you for wrong answers, so in such cases *only*, you may not want to guess unless you have some basis for your answer.

7) Suggestions
   a. Objective-type questions
      1. Examine the question booklet for proper sequence of pages and questions
      2. Read all instructions carefully
      3. Skip any question which seems too difficult; return to it after all other questions have been answered
      4. Apportion your time properly; do not spend too much time on any single question or group of questions

5. Note and underline key words – *all, most, fewest, least, best, worst, same, opposite*, etc.
6. Pay particular attention to negatives
7. Note unusual option, e.g., unduly long, short, complex, different or similar in content to the body of the question
8. Observe the use of "hedging" words – *probably, may, most likely*, etc.
9. Make sure that your answer is put next to the same number as the question
10. Do not second-guess unless you have good reason to believe the second answer is definitely more correct
11. Cross out original answer if you decide another answer is more accurate; do not erase until you are ready to hand your paper in
12. Answer all questions; guess unless instructed otherwise
13. Leave time for review

   b. Essay questions
      1. Read each question carefully
      2. Determine exactly what is wanted. Underline key words or phrases.
      3. Decide on outline or paragraph answer
      4. Include many different points and elements unless asked to develop any one or two points or elements
      5. Show impartiality by giving pros and cons unless directed to select one side only
      6. Make and write down any assumptions you find necessary to answer the questions
      7. Watch your English, grammar, punctuation and choice of words
      8. Time your answers; don't crowd material

8) Answering the essay question

Most essay questions can be answered by framing the specific response around several key words or ideas. Here are a few such key words or ideas:

M's: manpower, materials, methods, money, management
P's: purpose, program, policy, plan, procedure, practice, problems, pitfalls, personnel, public relations

   a. Six basic steps in handling problems:
      1. Preliminary plan and background development
      2. Collect information, data and facts
      3. Analyze and interpret information, data and facts
      4. Analyze and develop solutions as well as make recommendations
      5. Prepare report and sell recommendations
      6. Install recommendations and follow up effectiveness

   b. Pitfalls to avoid
      1. *Taking things for granted* – A statement of the situation does not necessarily imply that each of the elements is necessarily true; for example, a complaint may be invalid and biased so that all that can be taken for granted is that a complaint has been registered

2. *Considering only one side of a situation* – Wherever possible, indicate several alternatives and then point out the reasons you selected the best one
3. *Failing to indicate follow up* – Whenever your answer indicates action on your part, make certain that you will take proper follow-up action to see how successful your recommendations, procedures or actions turn out to be
4. *Taking too long in answering any single question* – Remember to time your answers properly

IX. AFTER THE TEST

Scoring procedures differ in detail among civil service jurisdictions although the general principles are the same. Whether the papers are hand-scored or graded by machine we have described, they are nearly always graded by number. That is, the person who marks the paper knows only the number – never the name – of the applicant. Not until all the papers have been graded will they be matched with names. If other tests, such as training and experience or oral interview ratings have been given, scores will be combined. Different parts of the examination usually have different weights. For example, the written test might count 60 percent of the final grade, and a rating of training and experience 40 percent. In many jurisdictions, veterans will have a certain number of points added to their grades.

After the final grade has been determined, the names are placed in grade order and an eligible list is established. There are various methods for resolving ties between those who get the same final grade – probably the most common is to place first the name of the person whose application was received first. Job offers are made from the eligible list in the order the names appear on it. You will be notified of your grade and your rank as soon as all these computations have been made. This will be done as rapidly as possible.

People who are found to meet the requirements in the announcement are called "eligibles." Their names are put on a list of eligible candidates. An eligible's chances of getting a job depend on how high he stands on this list and how fast agencies are filling jobs from the list.

When a job is to be filled from a list of eligibles, the agency asks for the names of people on the list of eligibles for that job. When the civil service commission receives this request, it sends to the agency the names of the three people highest on this list. Or, if the job to be filled has specialized requirements, the office sends the agency the names of the top three persons who meet these requirements from the general list.

The appointing officer makes a choice from among the three people whose names were sent to him. If the selected person accepts the appointment, the names of the others are put back on the list to be considered for future openings.

That is the rule in hiring from all kinds of eligible lists, whether they are for typist, carpenter, chemist, or something else. For every vacancy, the appointing officer has his choice of any one of the top three eligibles on the list. This explains why the person whose name is on top of the list sometimes does not get an appointment when some of the persons lower on the list do. If the appointing officer chooses the second or third eligible, the No. 1 eligible does not get a job at once, but stays on the list until he is appointed or the list is terminated.

X. HOW TO PASS THE INTERVIEW TEST

The examination for which you applied requires an oral interview test. You have already taken the written test and you are now being called for the interview test – the final part of the formal examination.

You may think that it is not possible to prepare for an interview test and that there are no procedures to follow during an interview. Our purpose is to point out some things you can do in advance that will help you and some good rules to follow and pitfalls to avoid while you are being interviewed.

What is an interview supposed to test?

The written examination is designed to test the technical knowledge and competence of the candidate; the oral is designed to evaluate intangible qualities, not readily measured otherwise, and to establish a list showing the relative fitness of each candidate – as measured against his competitors – for the position sought. Scoring is not on the basis of "right" and "wrong," but on a sliding scale of values ranging from "not passable" to "outstanding." As a matter of fact, it is possible to achieve a relatively low score without a single "incorrect" answer because of evident weakness in the qualities being measured.

Occasionally, an examination may consist entirely of an oral test – either an individual or a group oral. In such cases, information is sought concerning the technical knowledges and abilities of the candidate, since there has been no written examination for this purpose. More commonly, however, an oral test is used to supplement a written examination.

Who conducts interviews?

The composition of oral boards varies among different jurisdictions. In nearly all, a representative of the personnel department serves as chairman. One of the members of the board may be a representative of the department in which the candidate would work. In some cases, "outside experts" are used, and, frequently, a businessman or some other representative of the general public is asked to serve. Labor and management or other special groups may be represented. The aim is to secure the services of experts in the appropriate field.

However the board is composed, it is a good idea (and not at all improper or unethical) to ascertain in advance of the interview who the members are and what groups they represent. When you are introduced to them, you will have some idea of their backgrounds and interests, and at least you will not stutter and stammer over their names.

What should be done before the interview?

While knowledge about the board members is useful and takes some of the surprise element out of the interview, there is other preparation which is more substantive. It *is* possible to prepare for an oral interview – in several ways:

1) Keep a copy of your application and review it carefully before the interview

This may be the only document before the oral board, and the starting point of the interview. Know what education and experience you have listed there, and the sequence and dates of all of it. Sometimes the board will ask you to review the highlights of your experience for them; you should not have to hem and haw doing it.

2) Study the class specification and the examination announcement

Usually, the oral board has one or both of these to guide them. The qualities, characteristics or knowledges required by the position sought are stated in these documents. They offer valuable clues as to the nature of the oral interview. For example, if the job involves supervisory responsibilities, the announcement will usually indicate that knowledge of modern supervisory methods and the qualifications of the candidate as a supervisor will be tested. If so, you can expect such questions, frequently in the form of a hypothetical situation which you are expected to solve. NEVER go into an oral without knowledge of the duties and responsibilities of the job you seek.

3) Think through each qualification required

Try to visualize the kind of questions you would ask if you were a board member. How well could you answer them? Try especially to appraise your own knowledge and background in each area, *measured against the job sought*, and identify any areas in which you are weak. Be critical and realistic – do not flatter yourself.

4) Do some general reading in areas in which you feel you may be weak

For example, if the job involves supervision and your past experience has NOT, some general reading in supervisory methods and practices, particularly in the field of human relations, might be useful. Do NOT study agency procedures or detailed manuals. The oral board will be testing your understanding and capacity, not your memory.

5) Get a good night's sleep and watch your general health and mental attitude

You will want a clear head at the interview. Take care of a cold or any other minor ailment, and of course, no hangovers.

What should be done on the day of the interview?

Now comes the day of the interview itself. Give yourself plenty of time to get there. Plan to arrive somewhat ahead of the scheduled time, particularly if your appointment is in the fore part of the day. If a previous candidate fails to appear, the board might be ready for you a bit early. By early afternoon an oral board is almost invariably behind schedule if there are many candidates, and you may have to wait. Take along a book or magazine to read, or your application to review, but leave any extraneous material in the waiting room when you go in for your interview. In any event, relax and compose yourself.

The matter of dress is important. The board is forming impressions about you – from your experience, your manners, your attitude, and your appearance. Give your personal appearance careful attention. Dress your best, but not your flashiest. Choose conservative, appropriate clothing, and be sure it is immaculate. This is a business interview, and your appearance should indicate that you regard it as such. Besides, being well groomed and properly dressed will help boost your confidence.

Sooner or later, someone will call your name and escort you into the interview room. *This is it.* From here on you are on your own. It is too late for any more preparation. But remember, you asked for this opportunity to prove your fitness, and you are here because your request was granted.

What happens when you go in?

The usual sequence of events will be as follows: The clerk (who is often the board stenographer) will introduce you to the chairman of the oral board, who will introduce you to the other members of the board. Acknowledge the introductions before you sit down. Do not be surprised if you find a microphone facing you or a stenotypist sitting by. Oral interviews are usually recorded in the event of an appeal or other review.

Usually the chairman of the board will open the interview by reviewing the highlights of your education and work experience from your application – primarily for the benefit of the other members of the board, as well as to get the material into the record. Do not interrupt or comment unless there is an error or significant misinterpretation; if that is the case, do not hesitate. But do not quibble about insignificant matters. Also, he will usually ask you some question about your education, experience or your present job – partly to get you to start talking and to establish the interviewing "rapport." He may start the actual questioning, or turn it over to one of the other members. Frequently, each member undertakes the questioning on a particular area, one in which he is perhaps most competent, so you can expect each member to participate in the examination. Because time is limited, you may also expect some rather abrupt switches in the direction the questioning takes, so do not be upset by it. Normally, a board member will not pursue a single line of questioning unless he discovers a particular strength or weakness.

After each member has participated, the chairman will usually ask whether any member has any further questions, then will ask you if you have anything you wish to add. Unless you are expecting this question, it may floor you. Worse, it may start you off on an extended, extemporaneous speech. The board is not usually seeking more information. The question is principally to offer you a last opportunity to present further qualifications or to indicate that you have nothing to add. So, if you feel that a significant qualification or characteristic has been overlooked, it is proper to point it out in a sentence or so. Do not compliment the board on the thoroughness of their examination – they have been sketchy, and you know it. If you wish, merely say, "No thank you, I have nothing further to add." This is a point where you can "talk yourself out" of a good impression or fail to present an important bit of information. Remember, *you close the interview yourself.*

The chairman will then say, "That is all, Mr. _____, thank you." Do not be startled; the interview is over, and quicker than you think. Thank him, gather your belongings and take your leave. Save your sigh of relief for the other side of the door.

How to put your best foot forward

Throughout this entire process, you may feel that the board individually and collectively is trying to pierce your defenses, seek out your hidden weaknesses and embarrass and confuse you. Actually, this is not true. They are obliged to make an appraisal of your qualifications for the job you are seeking, and they want to see you in your best light. Remember, they must interview all candidates and a non-cooperative candidate may become a failure in spite of their best efforts to bring out his qualifications. Here are 15 suggestions that will help you:

1) Be natural – Keep your attitude confident, not cocky

If you are not confident that you can do the job, do not expect the board to be. Do not apologize for your weaknesses, try to bring out your strong points. The board is interested in a positive, not negative, presentation. Cockiness will antagonize any board member and make him wonder if you are covering up a weakness by a false show of strength.

2) Get comfortable, but don't lounge or sprawl

Sit erectly but not stiffly. A careless posture may lead the board to conclude that you are careless in other things, or at least that you are not impressed by the importance of the occasion. Either conclusion is natural, even if incorrect. Do not fuss with your clothing, a pencil or an ashtray. Your hands may occasionally be useful to emphasize a point; do not let them become a point of distraction.

3) Do not wisecrack or make small talk

This is a serious situation, and your attitude should show that you consider it as such. Further, the time of the board is limited – they do not want to waste it, and neither should you.

4) Do not exaggerate your experience or abilities
In the first place, from information in the application or other interviews and sources, the board may know more about you than you think. Secondly, you probably will not get away with it. An experienced board is rather adept at spotting such a situation, so do not take the chance.

5) If you know a board member, do not make a point of it, yet do not hide it
Certainly you are not fooling him, and probably not the other members of the board. Do not try to take advantage of your acquaintanceship – it will probably do you little good.

6) Do not dominate the interview
Let the board do that. They will give you the clues – do not assume that you have to do all the talking. Realize that the board has a number of questions to ask you, and do not try to take up all the interview time by showing off your extensive knowledge of the answer to the first one.

7) Be attentive
You only have 20 minutes or so, and you should keep your attention at its sharpest throughout. When a member is addressing a problem or question to you, give him your undivided attention. Address your reply principally to him, but do not exclude the other board members.

8) Do not interrupt
A board member may be stating a problem for you to analyze. He will ask you a question when the time comes. Let him state the problem, and wait for the question.

9) Make sure you understand the question
Do not try to answer until you are sure what the question is. If it is not clear, restate it in your own words or ask the board member to clarify it for you. However, do not haggle about minor elements.

10) Reply promptly but not hastily
A common entry on oral board rating sheets is "candidate responded readily," or "candidate hesitated in replies." Respond as promptly and quickly as you can, but do not jump to a hasty, ill-considered answer.

11) Do not be peremptory in your answers
A brief answer is proper – but do not fire your answer back. That is a losing game from your point of view. The board member can probably ask questions much faster than you can answer them.

12) Do not try to create the answer you think the board member wants
He is interested in what kind of mind you have and how it works – not in playing games. Furthermore, he can usually spot this practice and will actually grade you down on it.

13) Do not switch sides in your reply merely to agree with a board member
Frequently, a member will take a contrary position merely to draw you out and to see if you are willing and able to defend your point of view. Do not start a debate, yet do not surrender a good position. If a position is worth taking, it is worth defending.

14) Do not be afraid to admit an error in judgment if you are shown to be wrong

The board knows that you are forced to reply without any opportunity for careful consideration. Your answer may be demonstrably wrong. If so, admit it and get on with the interview.

15) Do not dwell at length on your present job

The opening question may relate to your present assignment. Answer the question but do not go into an extended discussion. You are being examined for a *new* job, not your present one. As a matter of fact, try to phrase ALL your answers in terms of the job for which you are being examined.

Basis of Rating

Probably you will forget most of these "do's" and "don'ts" when you walk into the oral interview room. Even remembering them all will not ensure you a passing grade. Perhaps you did not have the qualifications in the first place. But remembering them will help you to put your best foot forward, without treading on the toes of the board members.

Rumor and popular opinion to the contrary notwithstanding, an oral board wants you to make the best appearance possible. They know you are under pressure – but they also want to see how you respond to it as a guide to what your reaction would be under the pressures of the job you seek. They will be influenced by the degree of poise you display, the personal traits you show and the manner in which you respond.

ABOUT THIS BOOK

This book contains tests divided into Examination Sections. Go through each test, answering every question in the margin. We have also attached a sample answer sheet at the back of the book that can be removed and used. At the end of each test look at the answer key and check your answers. On the ones you got wrong, look at the right answer choice and learn. Do not fill in the answers first. Do not memorize the questions and answers, but understand the answer and principles involved. On your test, the questions will likely be different from the samples. Questions are changed and new ones added. If you understand these past questions you should have success with any changes that arise. Tests may consist of several types of questions. We have additional books on each subject should more study be advisable or necessary for you. Finally, the more you study, the better prepared you will be. This book is intended to be the last thing you study before you walk into the examination room. Prior study of relevant texts is also recommended. NLC publishes some of these in our Fundamental Series. Knowledge and good sense are important factors in passing your exam. Good luck also helps. So now study this Passbook, absorb the material contained within and take that knowledge into the examination. Then do your best to pass that exam.

EXAMINATION SECTION

EXAMINATION SECTION
TEST 1

DIRECTIONS: Each question or incomplete statement is followed by several suggested answers or completions. Select the one that BEST answers the question or completes the statement. *PRINT THE LETTER OF THE CORRECT ANSWER IN THE SPACE AT THE RIGHT.*

1. Computer graphic programming is concerned with
   A. animation
   B. pixel addressing
   C. color representation
   D. all of the above

   1.____

2. DIB is an abbreviation for
   A. data input button
   B. data dependent bitmap
   C. device independent bitmap
   D. none of the above

   2.____

3. Computer graphics can be categorized into
   A. real time
   B. interactive
   C. photo-realistic
   D. all of the above

   3.____

4. DIB are used as native graphics for
   A. Windows Embedded CE
   B. Directx
   C. both A and B
   D. none of the above

   4.____

5. An image is _____ of pixel which varies in colors.
   A. triangle
   B. rectangle
   C. circle
   D. all of the above

   5.____

6. Graphic software deals with
   A. images
   B. animations
   C. architecture
   D. all of the above

   6.____

7. Skencil is a program which is developed for
   A. Unix
   B. Linux
   C. none of the above
   D. both A and B

   7.____

8. 3D Plus is suitable for _____ jobs.
   A. small
   B. quick
   C. long
   D. all of the above

   8.____

9. An important characteristic of digital cameras is
   A. speed
   B. portability
   C. non-contact digitizing
   D. all of the above

   9.____

10. Snap is a function of AutoCAD which is used to _____ fixed points.   10._____
    A. add   B. delete
    C. maintain   D. all of the above

11. Engineering drawings include   11._____
    A. isometric   B. orthographic
    C. dimensioning   D. all of the above

12. Drafting is another name of _____ drawing.   12._____
    A. technical   B. engineering
    C. complex   D. all of the above

13. Architectural models represent _____ design.   13._____
    A. technical   B. engineering
    C. architectural   D. none of the above

14. Base maps represent physical features like   14._____
    A. street grids   B. river locations
    C. landscapes   D. all of the above

15. Two major types of base maps are   15._____
    A. skeleton base maps   B. country and township base maps
    C. interior maps   D. A and B only

16. Abstraction is the most important phase in the _____ process.   16._____
    A. development   B. design
    C. both A and B   D. none of the above

17. In the design process, _____ helps in redesigning.   17._____
    A. abstraction   B. models
    C. simulation   D. all of the above

18. Prerequisites for logical design are   18._____
    A. business analysis   B. technical requirements
    C. both A and B   D. none of the above

19. A graphics technician maintains records in the form of   19._____
    A. print orders   B. billing files
    C. maintenance agreements   D. all of the above

20. Technical drawing requires intensive   20._____
    A. communication   B. expertise
    C. both A and B   D. none of the above

21. A computer graphic technician is responsible for   21._____
    A. concepts   B. interpretation of design
    C. both A and B   D. none of the above

22. A computer graphic technician deals with
    A. advertising
    B. marketing
    C. multimedia publishing
    D. all of the above

    22.____

23. A graphic technician should have communication with a
    A. graphic designer
    B. requirement engineer
    C. project manager
    D. all of the above

    23.____

24. Interdisciplinary environment is important for a
    A. graphic technician
    B. graphic designer
    C. none of the above
    D. both A and B

    24.____

25. A graphic technician must be
    A. a team player
    B. challenging
    C. innovative
    D. all of the above

    25.____

KEY (CORRECT ANSWERS)

1. D
2. C
3. D
4. C
5. B

6. D
7. D
8. A
9. D
10. A

11. D
12. A
13. C
14. D
15. D

16. B
17. C
18. C
19. D
20. A

21. C
22. D
23. D
24. A
25. D

TEST 2

DIRECTIONS: Each question or incomplete statement is followed by several suggested answers or completions. Select the one that BEST answers the question or completes the statement. *PRINT THE LETTER OF THE CORRECT ANSWER IN THE SPACE AT THE RIGHT.*

1. Visual unity is a basic goal for _____ design. 1._____
   A. graphic   B. web
   C. architecture   D. both A and B

2. _____ is an important element of good graphic design. 2._____
   A. color   B. hierarchy
   C. image   D. all of the above

3. Graphics designing is based on _____ of design. 3._____
   A. elements   B. principles
   C. none of the above D. both A and B

4. Normally there are _____ elements of design. 4._____
   A. 5   B. 2
   C. 6   D. none of the above

5. Proximity is part of _____ of design. 5._____
   A. principles   B. elements
   C. none of the above D. both A and B

6. Computer graphics can be divided into _____ groups. 6._____
   A. 2   B. 6   C. 5   D. 3

7. The basic shapes used in graphic design are 7._____
   A. circle   B. square
   C. triangle   D. all of the above

8. Positive and negative space must be considered in every 8._____
   A. concept   B. design
   C. element   D. none of the above

9. _____ is the critical aspect of graphic design. 9._____
   A. Size   B. Shape
   C. Color   D. None of the above

10. Graphical representations are _____ of textual content. 10._____
    A. images   B. illustrations
    C. both A and B   D. all of the above

11. An architectural model is a(n) _____ model.
    A. engineering
    B. complex
    C. scale
    D. all of the above

    11._____

12. Presentation, fundraising, and obtaining permits can be shown by a(n) _____ model.
    A. software
    B. engineering
    C. architectural
    D. all of the above

    12._____

13. Urban models are one of the _____ models.
    A. engineering
    B. scientific
    C. architectural
    D. none of the above

    13._____

14. In industry and engineering, ideas are represented by
    A. design
    B. images
    C. technical drawings
    D. none of the above

    14._____

15. Computer aided designs are of _____ types.
    A. five
    B. two
    C. three
    D. none of the above

    15._____

16. _____ graphics are the easy way to present complex technical information.
    A. technical
    B. simple
    C. complex
    D. all of the above

    16._____

17. _____ is an architecture design software.
    A. Photoshop
    B. Sketch Up
    C. None of the above
    D. Both A and B

    17._____

18. Translating complex drawings into creative models is a(n) _____ task.
    A. challenging
    B. innovative
    C. important
    D. all of the above

    18._____

19. Drawing tools assist in
    A. layout
    B. speed
    C. both A and B
    D. none of the above

    19._____

20. Technical drawings can BEST be drawn by
    A. Autodesk
    B. Softimage
    C. both A and B
    D. none of the above

    20._____

21. A graphic technician must have _____ skills.
    A. technical
    B. design
    C. both A and B
    D. none of the above

    21._____

22. Information communication can help in resolving complex _____ issues.
    A. design
    B. technical
    C. architectural
    D. all of the above

    22._____

23. A graphic technician collaborates with
    A. a team
    B. stakeholders
    C. technical persons
    D. all of the above

24. _____ are also prepared by a graphic technician.
    A. Presentations
    B. Bitmap
    C. None of the above
    D. Both A and B

25. A graphic technician works under the supervision of
    A. an engineer
    B. architect
    C. graphic supervisor
    D. all of the above

KEY (CORRECT ANSWERS)

1.	A	11.	C
2.	B	12.	C
3.	D	13.	C
4.	C	14.	C
5.	A	15.	B
6.	A	16.	B
7.	D	17.	B
8.	B	18.	D
9.	C	19.	C
10.	A	20.	A

21. C
22. D
23. D
24. A
25. C

TEST 3

DIRECTIONS: Each question or incomplete statement is followed by several suggested answers or completions. Select the one that BEST answers the question or completes the statement. *PRINT THE LETTER OF THE CORRECT ANSWER IN THE SPACE AT THE RIGHT.*

1. Graphic representations include
   A. concept maps
   B. comparison
   C. process
   D. all of the above

   1.____

2. Similarity is an important concern of design
   A. principle
   B. web designer
   C. computer graphic technician
   D. A and B only

   2.____

3. 3D computer graphics depend on _____ images.
   A. raster
   B. vector
   C. bitmap
   D. both A and B

   3.____

4. A three-dimensional object can be represented by a(n) _____ model.
   A. 3D
   B. technical
   C. engineering
   D. all of the above

   4.____

5. _____ is the best way to convert a model into an image.
   A. Drafting
   B. Rendering
   C. Drawing
   D. All of the above

   5.____

6. 3D modeling software includes
   A. Blender
   B. Art of Illusion
   C. Softimage
   D. all of the above

   6.____

7. AutoCAD is concerned with
   A. drafting
   B. developing
   C. customizing
   D. all of the above

   7.____

8. To open a 2D drawing in a 3D program, _____ file extension works well.
   A. DWG
   B. GIF
   C. PNG
   D. all of the above

   8.____

9. Paper design is replaced by
   A. AutoCAD
   B. Microstation
   C. none of the above
   D. both A and B

   9.____

10. _____ demonstrates 2D and 3D modeling.
    A. Drafting
    B. Designing
    C. None of the above
    D. All of the above

    10.____

7

11. Architects use architectural models because models provide
    A. quick understanding   B. efficiency
    C. easy demonstration   D. all of the above

11._____

12. Which of the following types of model is normally used for landscape modeling?
    A. Interior model   B. Exterior model
    C. Urban model   D. All of the above

12._____

13. Prototyping technologies are normally _____ based.
    A. modeling   B. Photoshop
    C. CAD   D. all of the above

13._____

14. In an isometric model, object lines are always drawn
    A. vertically   B. horizontally
    C. parallel   D. all of the above

14._____

15. Hidden components of a device are shown by _____ through technical drawing.
    A. AutoCAD   B. Cross-sectional view
    C. Both A and B   D. none of the above

15._____

16. A technical drawing has _____ basic applications.
    A. two   B. five
    C. three   D. none of the above

16._____

17. Full section view in architectural design is known as
    A. dimension   B. plan
    C. axis   D. all of the above

17._____

18. Engineering drawings are concerned with
    A. layout   B. interpretation
    C. appearance   A. all of the above

18._____

19. Two types of technical drawings which are based on graphic projection are
    A. two-dimensional representation   B. three-dimensional representation
    C. both A and B   D. none of the above

19._____

20. Interior models are concerned with
    A. space planning   B. furniture
    C. colors   D. all of the above

20._____

21. A graphic technician should be aware of
    A. principles   B. processes
    C. equipment   D. all of the above

21._____

22. Interpersonal skills are important to learn for
 A. graphics technician B. web designer
 C. project manager D. all of the above

23. Record keeping techniques are defined by
 A. stakeholders B. graphic designers
 C. graphic technicians D. all of the above

24. Maintenance of equipment is important to keep
 A. data B. records
 C. none of the above D. both A and B

25. _____ communication is an important concern of the design phase.
 A. Oral B. Written
 C. Both A and B D. None of the above

KEY (CORRECT ANSWERS)

1. D 11. D
2. A 12. B
3. D 13. C
4. A 14. A
5. B 15. B

6. D 16. A
7. D 17. B
8. A 18. D
9. D 19. C
10. A 20. D

21. D
22. D
23. C
24. B
25. D

TEST 4

DIRECTIONS: Each question or incomplete statement is followed by several suggested answers or completions. Select the one that BEST answers the question or completes the statement. *PRINT THE LETTER OF THE CORRECT ANSWER IN THE SPACE AT THE RIGHT.*

1. Design elements include
   A. attributes
   B. shapes
   C. architecture
   D. all of the above

   1._____

2. Tactile texture provides _____ dimensional impression of the surface.
   A. two
   B. three
   C. one
   D. all of the above

   2._____

3. Space is an important concern of design which includes
   A. overlap
   B. shading
   C. highlight
   D. all of the above

   3._____

4. Repetition and continuation are methods of _____ design.
   A. elements
   B. both A and C
   C. principles
   D. all of the above

   4._____

5. Direction and texture are _____ of design.
   A. elements
   B. rules
   C. both A and B
   D. all of the above

   5._____

6. Architecture design is handled through
   A. CAD
   B. CAAD
   C. AutoCAD
   D. all of the above

   6._____

7. _____ is used for 3D architecture of homes.
   A. Photoshop
   B. Autodesk
   C. Chief architect
   D. All of the above

   7._____

8. Autodesk has the ability to provide
   A. innovation
   B. visualization
   C. simulation
   D. all of the above

   8._____

9. Building information modeling is the modern drift in
   A. architecture
   B. engineering
   C. construction
   D. all of the above

   9._____

10. _____ is a software tool for business information modeling.
    A. Archicad
    B. AutoCAD
    C. Illustrator
    D. All of the above

    10._____

11. Home, kitchen, baths, and interiors are BEST designed by
    A. home designer suit
    B. Archicad
    C. both A and B
    D. all of the above
    11.____

12. When CAD is used for mechanical designs, _____ based graphics are preferred.
    A. raster
    B. vector
    C. both A and B
    D. all of the above
    12.____

13. CAD is also used in industrial
    A. aerospace
    B. automotives
    C. shipbuilding
    D. all of the above
    13.____

14. Animations can also be created by using
    A. Photoshop
    B. CAD
    C. Flash
    D. all of the above
    14.____

15. Photo simulations are prepared by using
    A. Photoshop
    B. CAD
    C. CAAD
    D. both A and B
    15.____

16. 3D wireframe is an extension of _____ drafting.
    A. 2D
    B. 3D
    C. linear
    D. all of the above
    16.____

17. AutoCAD software for 2D drafting provides
    A. customization
    B. quick design
    C. precise templates
    D. all of the above
    17.____

18. _____ is concerned with design blueprints.
    A. CAD pro technical drawing
    B. Softimage
    C. Edraw
    D. None of the above
    18.____

19. Speed, efficiency, and portability are benefits of
    A. AutoCAD
    B. CAD pro technical drawing
    C. both A and B
    D. none of the above
    19.____

20. Detailed technical drawings always save
    A. time
    B. cost
    C. both A and B
    D. none of the above
    20.____

21. Engineers and designers mostly use _____ to create 3D models.
    A. Solid Edge 2D Drafting
    B. Blender
    C. BRL-CAD
    D. none of the above
    21.____

22. The most famous 2D CAD software is
    A. FreeCAD
    B. Photoshop
    C. AutoCAD
    D. all of the above

22.____

23. K3DSurf is used to draw
    A. mathematic models
    B. engineering
    C. architectural
    D. all of the above

23.____

24. Graphic technician concerns _____ to prepare designs.
    A. graphic designer
    B. technical persons
    C. team leaders
    D. all of the above

24.____

25. Patent designs are BEST handled by
    A. AutoCAD
    B. CAD Pro
    C. Blender
    D. all of the above

25.____

KEY (CORRECT ANSWERS)

1.	D		11.	A
2.	B		12.	B
3.	D		13.	D
4.	C		14.	D
5.	A		15.	B
6.	B		16.	A
7.	C		17.	D
8.	D		18.	A
9.	D		19.	B
10.	A		20.	C

21.	A
22.	C
23.	A
24.	D
25.	B

EXAMINATION SECTION
TEST 1

DIRECTIONS: Each question or incomplete statement is followed by several suggested answers or completions. Select the one that BEST answers the question or completes the statement. *PRINT THE LETTER OF THE CORRECT ANSWER IN THE SPACE AT THE RIGHT.*

1. A computer graphics specialist may NOT work with
   A. modeling and transformations
   B. rendering techniques
   C. OpenGL
   D. script writing

   1.____

2. Computer graphics specialists will NOT make
   A. 3D animations
   B. cartoons
   C. topographic maps
   D. graphics software

   2.____

3. CMYK is a(n) _____ model based on light reflected from white surfaces.
   A. light block
   B. additive
   C. subtractive
   D. luminosity-based

   3.____

4. Vector graphics use _____ in a work plane to represent images in computer graphics.
   A. vectors   B. lines   C. polygons   D. points

   4.____

5. Vector art is preferred because
   A. the image can be resized without loss of quality
   B. the image can be converted to bitmaps easily
   C. such a graphic uses less storage space
   D. the graphic is not dependent on the medium used

   5.____

6. A vector file is also called a _____ file.
   A. bitmap   B. geometric   C. raster   D. polygon

   6.____

7. A raster graphics image is comprised of
   A. vectors   B. image areas   C. bitmaps   D. lines

   7.____

8. Animation images will normally be
   A. JPEG files
   B. binary images
   C. database records
   D. vector files

   8.____

9. Which of the following is a vector format?
   A. Autocad DXF
   B. JPEG2000
   C. Esri TIN
   D. GeoTIF

   9.____

10. Graphic design does NOT include
    A. topography
    B. image-making
    C. typography
    D. color composition

    10.____

11. Which of the following is NOT a 3D animation application? 11._____
    A. 3DSMax B. Autocad C. Photoshop D. Maya

12. 3D printing is also known as 12._____
    A. fabrication
    B. additive manufacturing
    C. casting
    D. machining

13. Which of the following is NOT a core skill of a graphic designer? 13._____
    A. Topography B. Illustration C. Photography D. Animation

14. VRay, Mental ray are examples of modern 14._____
    A. render engines
    B. image editors
    C. illustrators
    D. visualization tools

15. DAZ3D does NOT provide support for 15._____
    A. scene building
    B. rigging
    C. modeling and texturing
    D. animation

16. Adobe After Effects is used for 16._____
    A. storyboarding
    B. movie effects
    C. photo effects
    D. rendering

17. MEL is a(n) _____ of MAYA. 17._____
    A. rendering engine
    B. core modeling tool
    C. scripting language
    D. animation library

18. AGAL is a(n) 18._____
    A. programming language
    B. API
    C. image converter
    D. game engine

19. Which of the following is NOT an example of 3D rendering software? 19._____
    A. 3D max B. AC3D C. V-Ray D. Adobe AIR

20. Autocad and Advance Steel are products of 20._____
    A. Autodesk B. Graphisoft C. DATACAD D. 4M

21. Which one of the following would you typically use for building a 3D architecture model? 21._____
    A. 3DS MAx B. AutoCAD C. CATIA D. CityEngine

22. GPU stands for 22._____
    A. Games Processing Unit
    B. General Process Uniformity
    C. Graphics Processing Unit
    D. None of the above

23. XNA is developed by Microsoft for games released on _____ platform. 23._____
    A. Xbox
    B. TorqueX
    C. Visual 3D.net
    D. Panda3D

24. Photo-realistic creatures look alive in _____ animation.   24._____
    A. character   B. creature   C. featured   D. human

25. True character animation started in   25._____
    A. 1914   B. 1969   C. 1984   D. 2003

KEY (CORRECT ANSWERS)

1. D
2. D
3. B
4. C
5. A

6. B
7. C
8. D
9. A
10. A

11. C
12. B
13. A
14. A
15. C

16. B
17. C
18. C
19. B
20. A

21. D
22. C
23. A
24. B
25. C

TEST 2

DIRECTIONS: Each question or incomplete statement is followed by several suggested answers or completions. Select the one that BEST answers the question or completes the statement. *PRINT THE LETTER OF THE CORRECT ANSWER IN THE SPACE AT THE RIGHT.*

1. 2D graphics are divided into _____ categories.
   A. one   B. two   C. three   D. four
   1._____

2. Which of the following is NOT a 3D graphics program?
   A. Blender   B. Adobe Photoshop
   C. 3D Studio Max   D. None of the above
   2._____

3. Rasterisation will convert _____ to _____.
   A. bitmaps; vectors   B. 3D images; 2D
   C. vector images; bitmaps   D. 2D images; binary storage files
   3._____

4. _____ is the process of truncating triangles to fill within viewable area.
   A. Clipping   B. Tweaking   C. Spinning   D. Culling
   4._____

5. Distance of the image will reduce the image quality. _____ is used to achieve the best fit with least compromise in quality.
   A. Environment mapping   B. Texture filtering
   C. Bump mapping   D. Manipulating level of detail
   5._____

6. Vector graphics typically use _____ for displaying digital image.
   A. triangles   B. polygons   C. rectangles   D. circles
   6._____

7. Transforming a raster graphic to vector graphic is
   A. vectorization   B. rasterization
   C. digitization   D. tweaking
   7._____

8. GIS stands for _____ Information System.
   A. Graphics   B. Geographic   C. Global   D. General
   8._____

9. _____ can be a good source for vectorization.
   A. Live portraits   B. Technical drawings/maps
   C. OCR   D. Bitmaps
   9._____

10. Which one of the following is a graphics-editing program?
    A. Adobe Illustrator   B. Corel Draw
    C. AutoCAD   D. Inkskape
    10._____

11. _____ is a Java-based cross platform graphics editor.
    A. ImageTracer   B. Corel Draw
    C. Adobe Illustrator   D. Macromedia freehand
    11._____

12. _____ means processing of different layers with distinct themes.
    A. Map overlaying B. Cartographic modeling
    C. Hydrological modeling D. Geostatistics

    12.____

13. Adding more color detail to a 3D model typically means
    A. correcting the perspective B. developing
    C. diffusing D. texture mapping

    13.____

14. _____ will be used to create interfaces for software applications.
    A. Renderers B. Image Editors
    C. Visualization tools D. Illustrators

    14.____

15. Intentionally applying noise to prevent undesired patterns, especially at low resolution, is known as
    A. tweaking B. dithering C. texturing D. scene building

    15.____

16. Adobe _____ is used for publishing online videos.
    A. Animate B. Movie Effects
    C. Photo Effects D. AIR

    16.____

17. MEL is a(n) _____ of MAYA.
    A. rendering engine B. core modeling tool
    C. scripting language D. animation library

    17.____

18. Acquiring the shape of real-world objects is known as 3D
    A. reconstruction B. calibration
    C. extraction D. molding

    18.____

19. Calculation of the difference between key frames in a computer animation is automatically done using
    A. morphing B. real-time rendering
    C. screening D. plotting

    19.____

20. For human viewing, an animation is done at _____ frames/second.
    A. 24 to 30 B. 30 to 60 C. 120 D. 180

    20.____

21. Computer Dreams is a(n)
    A. movie B. visualization technique
    C. animation process D. rendering technique

    21.____

22. Color management in computer graphics means
    A. device-dependent color presentation
    B. use of appropriate color model
    C. appropriate lighting
    D. texture management

    22.____

23. Graphical representation of data is called
    A. prototyping B. dashboarding
    C. infographics D. infologic

    23.____

24. _____ is small displacement of the original surface to make it appear more realistic.   24._____
    A. Polygon mapping
    B. Bump mapping
    C. Triangle mapping
    D. Etching

25. _____ is a graphic depiction of a drawing concept.   25._____
    A. Storyboard
    B. Concept diagram
    C. Illustration
    D. Sketch

KEY (CORRECT ANSWERS)

1.	B	11.	A
2.	B	12.	B
3.	C	13.	D
4.	A	14.	C
5.	B	15.	A
6.	B	16.	A
7.	A	17.	C
8.	B	18.	A
9.	D	19.	D
10.	C	20.	A

21.	A
22.	A
23.	C
24.	B
25.	C

TEST 3

DIRECTIONS: Each question or incomplete statement is followed by several suggested answers or completions. Select the one that BEST answers the question or completes the statement. *PRINT THE LETTER OF THE CORRECT ANSWER IN THE SPACE AT THE RIGHT.*

1. _____ involves removal of distortion in digital images.
   A. Anti-aliasing   B. Blending   C. Banding   D. Easing
   1.____

2. Users can view and zoom stationary objects in
   A. motion dynamics   B. update dynamics
   C. motion synthesis   D. video synthesis
   2.____

3. Simulation of real-world environment would be done using
   A. process control   B. model rendering
   C. 3D dynamics   D. cartography
   3.____

4. In _____, the user can change parameters of a visual object.
   A. offline plotting   B. interactive plotting
   C. interactive design   D. visual design
   4.____

5. When using data, _____ may NOT be the core job function of a graphic specialist.
   A. handling complex data structures   B. mathematical accuracy of data
   C. handling huge data volume   D. handling large images
   5.____

6. Handling of a(n) _____ is NOT the core function of a computer graphics specialist.
   A. image   B. maps   C. sound   D. animation
   6.____

7. A source image may NOT be the only thing to work with in a _____ project.
   A. drafting   B. CAD   C. animation   D. pixel art
   7.____

8. _____ bitmap images contain only black and white colors.
   A. Line art   B. Gray scale   C. Multi-tone   D. Pixel art
   8.____

9. Infographics represent
   A. terrain analysis   B. mathematical curves
   C. information visualization   D. architectural design
   9.____

10. Duotone images contain _____ colors.
    A. 2   B. 4   C. 8   D. more than 8
    10.____

11. Stop-motion technique has been replaced by
    A. topography   B. computer animation
    C. tweening   D. morphing
    11.____

12. A 3D representation of a physical model typically uses
    A. art of illusion
    B. wire-frame modeling
    C. graphic rendering
    D. CAM

13. Bitmap images are mapped to a
    A. linear array of pixels
    B. polygon
    C. grid
    D. color triangle

14. Objects in a vector image will be defined using
    A. pixels
    B. grids
    C. mathematical equations
    D. programmable scripts

15. Geometric primitives include
    A. points, lines and ellipses
    B. squares and rectangles
    C. points and pixels
    D. areas and curves

16. Position of a polygon is defined in database by its
    A. sides and vertices
    B. area overlapping with other objects
    C. direction of vector
    D. layer number

17. SVG stands for
    A. Scalable Vector Graphics
    B. Scalable Video Graphics
    C. Scalable Value Graph
    D. Serialized Video Generation

18. A vector image is comprised of
    A. pixel grids
    B. pixel areas
    C. polygons
    D. Bezier curves

19. _____ mapping involves adding features like color and dimensions to polygons in a 3D model.
    A. Diffuse   B. Height   C. Texture   D. Bump

20. _____ is any point in a raster image.
    A. Sample
    B. Mapping point
    C. Pixel
    D. Vertex

21. Which of the following file types has built-in animation capability?
    A. GIF   B. JPEG   C. BMP   D. TIFF

22. Autodesk Maya is NOT mainly for
    A. animation
    B. visual 3D effects
    C. video-game creation
    D. lighting

23. Shortest path calculations are typically done in _____ software.
    A. GIS   B. MIS   C. Animation   D. Rendering

24. Which of the following is NOT a way to represent 3D models?
    A. Polygonal modeling
    B. State transition modeling
    C. Curve modeling
    D. digital sculpting

    24._____

25. Utah _____ is known as a beginner's standard 3D model.
    A. Teapot
    B. Bunny
    C. Suzanne
    D. Cornell Box

    25._____

KEY (CORRECT ANSWERS)

1. A
2. D
3. D
4. B
5. B

6. C
7. B
8. A
9. C
10. A

11. B
12. B
13. C
14. C
15. A

16. B
17. A
18. D
19. C
20. C

21. A
22. C
23. A
24. B
25. A

TEST 4

DIRECTIONS: Each question or incomplete statement is followed by several suggested answers or completions. Select the one that BEST answers the question or completes the statement. *PRINT THE LETTER OF THE CORRECT ANSWER IN THE SPACE AT THE RIGHT.*

1. Which one of the following is NOT used for CAD? 1.____
   A. 3DS Max
   B. Adobe Illustrator
   C. Cinema 4D
   D. Maya

2. Which one of the following is primarily NOT for web design? 2.____
   A. Xara Web Designer
   B. Adobe After Effects
   C. Adobe Dreamweaver
   D. Netobjects Fusion

3. RGB and CMYK are _____ models, respectively. 3.____
   A. additive color and subtractive color
   B. subtractive color and additive color
   C. object and crude
   D. shape and form

4. Animation uses _____ images. 4.____
   A. static   B. dynamic   C. distorted   D. cyclic

5. To study the Geometry of Motion in mechanical objects, we use 5.____
   A. animation   B. modeling   C. dynamics   D. rigging

6. There are _____ distinct parts of a shadow. 6.____
   A. 2   B. 3   C. 4   D. 5

7. A three-dimensional surface is represented on a computer. What kind of model does it represent? 7.____
   A. Conceptual   B. 3D   C. Solid   D. Ambient

8. Using which of the following programs do we generate an image from a 3D solid model? 8.____
   A. Rendering   B. Morphing   C. Warping   D. Rastering

9. _____ process will prepare 3D mesh for animation. 9.____
   A. Tweaking   B. Rigging   C. Blending   D. Rendering

10. In _____, a 2D image is taken and mapped to a polygon. 10.____
    A. texturing   B. blending   C. warping   D. detailing

11. Visual effects are also referred to as 11.____
    A. SFX   B. RTX   C. VFX   D. MXF

12. Which of the following software platforms is NOT used for visual effects?
    A. 3D Equalizer   B. Final Cut Pro
    C. After Effects   D. AutoCAD

13. Which of the following is NOT primarily meant for design?
    A. 3DS Max   B. Corel Painter
    C. Illustrator D. Indesign

14. Diffraction occurs when light
    A. scatters in different directions   B. passes through the medium
    C. bends around the corners   D. is partially absorbed

15. In _____ design we focus on the possible uses of computer hardware and software that is user specific.
    A. interactive   B. interaction   C. structural   D. humanistic

16. Texture mapping adds _____, whereas Bump mapping adds surface roughness.
    A. shade   B. color   C. distance   D. tone

17. Which of the following does NOT relate to statistical data mapping?
    A. Spatial analysis   B. Geospatial analysis
    C. Geomatics   D. Rendering

18. _____ is a term used for making and using maps.
    A. GIS   B. Modeling   C. Morphism   D. Cartography

19. Which one of the following is NOT used for Computer Aided Designing?
    A. AutoCAD   B. MODO   C. Cinema 4D   D. V-Ray

20. _____ refers to steps used to create a 2D raster image from a 3D scene.
    A. Graphic transformation   B. Image buffering
    C. Tweaking   D. Anti-aliasing

21. _____ is to remove segments that are outside the viewing area.
    A. Linear transformation   B. Clipping
    C. Solid modeling   D. Rigging

22. Web browser engine renders
    A. digital image   B. HTML
    C. 2D image   D. 3D model

23. Real-time rendering is specific to
    A. hardware accelerators   B. extra memory resources
    C. high processing speeds   D. all of the above

24. Sprites are examples of
    A. polygons   B. primitives   C. graphics   D. triangles

25. _____ is a method for mapping 3D points to 2D planes.   25._____
   A. 3D projection   B. 2D projection
   C. Vector projection   D. Scene rendering

KEY (CORRECT ANSWERS)

1. B   11. C
2. B   12. D
3. A   13. A
4. A   14. C
5. C   15. A

6. B   16. B
7. C   17. D
8. A   18. D
9. B   19. B
10. A   20. A

21. B
22. B
23. A
24. B
25. A

EXAMINATION SECTION
TEST 1

DIRECTIONS: Each question or incomplete statement is followed by several suggested answers or completions. Select the one that BEST answers the question or completes the statement. *PRINT THE LETTER OF THE CORRECT ANSWER IN THE SPACE AT THE RIGHT.*

1. The basic data-entry units that make up a spreadsheet are called
   A. boxes B. cells C. sheets D. tabs

2. You are assigned the task of creating a brochure that includes descriptions and images of the seasonal amenities available to town residents. The best software to use to create this brochure is
   A. Microsoft PowerPoint
   B. Adobe InDesign
   C. Google Drive
   D. Adobe Acrobat

3. The term *duplex* refers to
   A. prints with more than two colors
   B. tabloid-style newspapers
   C. double-spaced printing
   D. two-sided printing

4. Copyright law should be considered when an editor is
   A. thinking of synonyms that would enhance a magazine piece
   B. searching for images to run in a blog post
   C. deciding whether or not to use an anonymous source
   D. all of the above

5. Libel and slander both relate to the spread of false information, but differ in that libelous statements are _____ and slanderous statements are _____.
   A. violent; threatening
   B. in newspapers; on the internet
   C. written; spoken
   D. spoken; written

6. The proofreading mark used to indicate that text or punctuation should be inserted in a particular place is called a(n)
   A. asterisk B. pound sign C. caret D. slash

7. A social media assistant is told to put up a Facebook post the day before a youth video-game tournament at the local library. To best promote the tournament and generate excitement, the body of the post should read
   A. "It's Gamer Day Eve! Come on down tomorrow for a fun-filled day playing your favorite games!"
   B. "VIDEO GAMES TOMORROW! SEE YOU THERE!!!"
   C. "GAME...ON!!! First annual City Library Gamer Day Tourney begins in T-minus 24 hours! See you at 10 a.m.!"
   D. "Mayor Johnson wishes all participants in tomorrow's Gamer Day Tourney at City Library the best of luck, and new high scores for all!"

8. It is your job to post videos on Instagram of the day's leading news stories. Each post must include an excerpt from the news article, and a short headline should appear as a banner over the footage.
Which of the following headlines is correct in both style and grammar?
   A. TOWN COUNSEL APPROVES PERMIT FOR NEW DISTILLERY
   B. TOWN COUNSEL ISSUES PERMIT FOR LOCAL BREWERY
   C. TOWN COUNCIL APPROVED PERMIT FOR NEW DISTILLERY
   D. TOWN COUNCIL ISSUES PERMIT FOR NEW DISTILLERY

8.____

9. To assure credibility and avoid hostility, a public relations specialist MUST
   A. make certain the message is truthful, not evasive or exaggerated
   B. make sure the message contains some dire consequences, if ignored
   C. repeat the message often enough to that it cannot be ignored
   D. try to reach as many people and groups as possible

9.____

10. The public relations specialist MUST be prepared to assume that members of an audience
    A. may have developed attitudes toward proposals, whether favorable, neutral or unfavorable
    B. will be immediately hostile
    C. will consider any proposals with an open mind
    D. will invariably need an introduction to the subject

10.____

11. To a copy editor, *slug* means
    A. first sentence of a story
    B. identification of a story
    C. size of type in which a story is to be set
    D. the story needs punch or drive

11.____

12. You are assigned to write the photo cutline for a cover story about new local shops in the Sunday Business section. The photo shows the owner of a new coffeehouse brewing espresso as a customer waits at the register.
The cutline should include all of the following information EXCEPT the
    A. name of the owner   B. location of the coffeehouse
    C. name of the coffeehouse   D. name of the customer

12.____

13. When covering political events, a group of reporters might distribute quotes and relevant information to a larger contingent of journalists. These reporters are called
    A. political correspondents   B. news desk reporters
    C. distributing journalists   D. pool reporters

13.____

14. The lede is the MOST important part of a news story.
It should
    A. attract the reader
    B. give all the facts immediately
    C. start with the source of the story
    D. start with the time of the story

14.____

15. There are several acceptable ways of writing a news story. 15.____
It should USUALLY be written
   A. as facts become known, regardless of chronology
   B. chronologically
   C. in order of decreasing importance or interest
   D. so that details come at the end

16. A reporter assigned to cover a scheduled broadcast speech GENERALLY 16.____
   A. gets shorthand notes afterwards
   B. takes shorthand notes himself
   C. receives an advance copy
   D. writes his story from the radio or television broadcast

17. A reporter is told that an interview has been set up for him for the next day with 17.____
an authority on earthquakes. He is given the name and affiliation of the
authority and the location and time of the interview.
His NEXT step is to
   A. bring along a seismology expert to the interview
   B. do research on seismology and get biographical data on the interviewee
   C. try to arrange a luncheon date with the interviewee
   D. verify time and place of interview

18. When a story is worth handling on a continuing basis, even if no added news is 18.____
available, a writer will be asked to
   A. call the sources on deadline and make sure no facts are changed
   B. rearrange the story, putting other details in the lead
   C. shorten the story
   D. write a *second day* lead

19. There are almost as many techniques of interviewing as there are interviewers. 19.____
Of the following, the LEAST objectionable method is to
   A. ask if interviewee minds being quoted
   B. make occasional notes as important topics come up
   C. take notes unobtrusively
   D. take shorthand notes of every word

20. There are many differences between feature and news stories. 20.____
The single MOST important difference is that
   A. features are longer than news stories
   B. features emphasize the unusual; news stories the significant
   C. features ignore facts that news stories cannot
   D. news stories are more timely than features

Questions 21-25.

DIRECTIONS: In each of Questions 21 through 25, only one of the four sentences conforms to standards of correct usage. The other three contain errors in grammar, diction or punctuation. Select the option in each question which conforms to standards of correct usage. Consider an option correct if it contains none of the errors mentioned above, even though there may be other correct ways of expressing the same thought.

21. A. Because he was ill was no excuse for his behavior.
    B. I insist that he see a lawyer before he goes to trial.
    C. He said "that he had not intended to go."
    D. He wasn't out of the office only three days.

21._____

22. A. He came to the station and pays a porter to carry his bags into the train.
    B. I should have liked to live in medieval times.
    C. My father was born in Linville. A little country town where everyone knows everyone else.
    D. The car, which is parked across the street, is disabled.

22._____

23. A. He asked the desk clerk for a clean, quiet, room.
    B. I expected James to be lonesome and that he would want to go home.
    C. I have stopped worrying because I have heard nothing further on the subject.
    D. If the board of directors controls the company, they may take actions which are disapproved by the stockholders.

23._____

24. A. Each of the players knew their place.
    B. He whom you saw on the stage is the son of an actor.
    C. Susan is the smartest of the twin sisters.
    D. Who ever thought of him winning both prizes?

24._____

25. A. An outstanding trait of early man was their reliance on omens.
    B. Because I had never been there before.
    C. Neither Mr. Jones nor Mr. Smith has completed his work.
    D. While eating my dinner, a dog came to the window.

25._____

KEY (CORRECT ANSWERS)

1.	B	11.	B
2.	B	12.	D
3.	D	13.	D
4.	B	14.	A
5.	C	15.	C
6.	C	16.	C
7.	C	17.	B
8.	D	18.	D
9.	A	19.	C
10.	A	20.	B

21. B
22. B
23. C
24. B
25. C

TEST 2

DIRECTIONS: Each question or incomplete statement is followed by several suggested answers or completions. Select the one that BEST answers the question or completes the statement. *PRINT THE LETTER OF THE CORRECT ANSWER IN THE SPACE AT THE RIGHT.*

1. In a pre-edited news article or press release, ____ indicates the end of text. 1.____
   A. -30-   B. -end-   C. stet   D. -XX-

2. The term *double truck* is used to describe 2.____
   A. a two-column headline
   B. the first page of the second section
   C. two adjacent pages made up as one
   D. two pictures combined into a single picture

3. To indicate that a correction should be ignored and text left as is, an editor should use the notation 3.____
   A. stet   B. as/is   C. -#-   D. check

4. As a copy editor, you are assigned to edit an article about the local high school football team's summer training camp. The lede of the article reads: 4.____
   "Practice makes perfect, and based on early showing at camp, Marlboro might be in line for its finest season in a decade."
   This article should be sent back to the writer for revisions because
   A. clichés should be avoided in news articles, especially in the lede
   B. technically it's not accurate that practice makes perfect
   C. few readers are familiar with the history of the team
   D. the opinion of the writer is not relevant in a news article

5. The terms *vector* and *PNG* refer to 5.____
   A. peripheral devices   B. the first word processors
   C. font packages   D. computer graphics

6. The technique of trimming a photo to be used in a news story is known as 6.____
   A. casting off   B. cropping   C. routing   D. scaling down

7. Which of the following fonts would be most suitable for use in the website version of a news article? 7.____
   A. Helvetica   B. Baskerville   C. Garamond   D. Comic Sans

8. If the same article from question #7 is to be read in the print edition of the newspaper, the most suitable serif font would be 8.____
   A. Arial   B. Times   C. Verdana   D. Copperplate

9. In typography, the number of points to an inch is APPROXIMATELY 9.____
   A. 12   B. 48   C. 72   D. 96

10. All variants of a particular type design are said to belong to the same 10.____
    A. family   B. font   C. quad   D. run

11. Old English is in a class of type known as
    A. black letter   B. italic   C. roman   D. script

12. Which of the following is a sans serif font?
    A. Baskerville   B. Bodoni   C. Verdana   D. Garamond

13. The one of the following that is NOT associated with typography is
    A. kerning   B. cropping   C. leading   D. tracking

14. Of the following, the term that is NOT associated with the printing process is
    A. collate   B. duplex   C. export   D. offset

15. A large capital letter used as block text at the start of a paragraph is called a
    A. letter block   B. drop cap   C. drophead   D. subhead

16. A method of printing in which a relief process is used is
    A. intaglio   B. letter press   C. lithography   D. offset

17. A screened engraving of a photograph is known as
    A. intaglio   B. letter press   C. lithography   D. offset

18. In typography, the term used for arranging type in lines so that all the lines in a column are even is
    A. conversion   B. furnishing   C. justifying   D. leading

19. The front page of THE NEW YORK TIMES most frequently exemplifies the make-up known as
    A. balanced   B. circus
    C. focus   D. hanging indentation

20. Information about a newspaper's publisher, offices and subscription rates are typically found
    A. on the editorial page   B. in the masthead
    C. beneath the lead story   D. in the classified section

21. The word *stet* tells the printer to
    A. capitalize all letters in the phrase
    B. omit the phrase
    C. reinstate the phrase marked out
    D. set the marked phrase in italics

22. In proofreading, the symbol ✓✓✓ indicates that the printer should
    A. check with original manuscript   B. correct faulty spacing
    C. insert quotation marks   D. straighten lines

23. A proofreader indicates a *bad* or defective letter by the symbol   23._____
    A. ✗   B. ☐   C. ↄ   D. #

24. The proofreading symbol meaning *close up partly but leave some space* is   24._____
    A. (/)   B. ⊙   C. ⌢#⌣   D. ☐

25. A proof containing the misspelling *Beleive* should be marked   25._____
    A. tr   B. wf   C. ⊙   D. ⌡

KEY (CORRECT ANSWERS)

1.	A	11.	A
2.	C	12.	C
3.	A	13.	B
4.	A	14.	C
5.	D	15.	B
6.	B	16.	B
7.	A	17.	A
8.	B	18.	C
9.	C	19.	A
10.	A	20.	B

21.	C
22.	B
23.	A
24.	C
25.	A

GRAPHIC ARTS

EXAMINATION SECTION
TEST 1

DIRECTIONS: Each question or incomplete statement is followed by several suggested answers or completions. Select the one that BEST answers the question or completes the statement. *PRINT THE LETTER OF THE CORRECT ANSWER IN THE SPACE AT THE RIGHT.*

1. The term mitography is synonymous with _____ printing.　　　　　　　　　　　　1._____
   - A. relief
   - B. lithographic
   - C. screen
   - D. intaglio

2. Photography is PRIMARILY used in _____ printing.　　　　　　　　　　　　　　　2._____
   - A. planographic
   - B. stencil
   - C. relief
   - D. silk screen

3. A good project for a beginning class in photography would be to make　　　　　　3._____
   - A. contact prints
   - B. enlargements
   - C. montages
   - D. murals

4. A linoleum block is used to reproduce a　　　　　　　　　　　　　　　　　　　4._____
   - A. dry point
   - B. line drawing
   - C. mezzotint
   - D. aquatint

5. The process of preparing a press to obtain the proper printing impression is referred to as　　　5._____
   - A. lock-up
   - B. paste-up
   - C. make-ready
   - D. make-up

6. The vehicle used in the manufacture of printing ink is　　　　　　　　　　　　　　6._____
   - A. pigment
   - B. varnish
   - C. dryer
   - D. alcohol

7. As an aid in accurately locating gauge pins on the platen press, the FIRST impression is always printed on　　　7._____
   - A. a sheet of thin scrap paper
   - B. a single sheet of bristol index
   - C. the tympan sheet
   - D. the proof press

8. A line on a dry point plate is made　　　　　　　　　　　　　　　　　　　　　8._____
   - A. with a bruin
   - B. by etching with acid
   - C. with a linoleum gouge
   - D. by scratching the surface with a needle

33

9. Lumarith is a material used to make a

   A. linoleum cut B. half-tone print
   C. dry point engraving D. metallic stamping

10. The guides MOST frequently used in silk screen printing are _____ guides.

    A. pin B. quad C. metal D. paper

11. Direct image plastiplates BEST serve to demonstrate _____ printing.

    A. relief B. intaglio
    C. planographic D. letterpress

12. In making a rubber stamp, the type impression is made

    A. on unvulcanized rubber B. on molding board
    C. on a mica base D. directly on the mount

13. Lithography is preferred in certain situations because

    A. it requires no make-ready
    B. oil and water do not mix
    C. it is a fast printing process
    D. various colored inks would be printed simultaneously

14. A doctor blade would be found on a

    A. rotogravure press B. letterpress
    C. offset press D. bookbinder's press

15. The wire stapler is used to make the _____ stitch.

    A. kettle B. smyth C. saddle D. in-and-out

16. Headband is BEST described as

    A. a decorative strip of cloth placed at both ends of a bound book
    B. the strip of cloth that helps strengthen the hinge of a book
    C. the outer binding
    D. the metallic stamped line

17. An edition bound book has a _____ cover.

    A. paper B. case C. plastic D. flexible

18. Of the following, the type that is classified as script is

    A. Century schoolbook B. Spartan
    C. Bernhard light D. Goudy oldstyle

19. The plan of work in typesetting is referred to as a

    A. copy fitting B. layout
    C. blue point D. working drawing

20. The paper BEST suited for the printing of a lunch ticket is _____ paper.

    A. bond B. antique C. index D. coated

21. A rubber stamp is an example of _____ printing. 21.____

    A. stencil   B. relief
    C. planographic   D. intaglio

22. In locking up a type form in the chase, the quoins are always placed 22.____

    A. above and below the form
    B. above and to the right of the form
    C. below and to the left of the form
    D. to the left and to the right of the form

23. Type forms are tied 23.____

    A. on the proof press   B. on the bank
    C. in the chase   D. in the galley

24. Capital letters are arranged alphabetically in the California Job case with the exception of the letters 24.____

    A. *E* and *O*   B. *J* and *U*   C. *J* and *T*   D. *T* and *U*

25. A line of type 3 1/2" in length is equal to _____ picas. 25.____

    A. 11   B. 15   C. 19   D. 21

KEY (CORRECT ANSWERS)

1.	C	11.	C
2.	A	12.	B
3.	A	13.	C
4.	B	14.	A
5.	C	15.	C
6.	B	16.	A
7.	C	17.	B
8.	D	18.	C
9.	C	19.	B
10.	D	20.	C

21. B
22. B
23. D
24. B
25. D

TEST 2

DIRECTIONS: Each question or incomplete statement is followed by several suggested answers or completions. Select the one that BEST answers the question or completes the statement. *PRINT THE LETTER OF THE CORRECT ANSWER IN THE SPACE AT THE RIGHT.*

1. If 10 point 3-em quads are not available, the spaces that can be used from the 30-point case are   1.___

    A. 5-em spaces B. 4-em spaces
    C. 3-em spaces D. em-quads

2. Of the following, the type face that is classified as modern is   2.___

    A. Bodoni   B. Cloister   C. Garamond   D. Cheltenham

3. In setting gauge pins for a 3" x 5" card, the MOST suitable arrangement of the pins is   3.___

    A. one to the left, bottom and right
    B. two to the left, bottom and right
    C. two to the left and one on the bottom
    D. one to the left and two on the bottom

4. In printing a business card, the form is placed in the chase with the head to the   4.___

    A. left   B. bottom   C. right   D. top

5. The principle of the lithographic printing process may be demonstrated by using _____ plates.   5.___

    A. direct image plasti-   B. washoff
    C. zinc   D. dycrill

6. In silk screen printing, a frisket is used   6.___

    A. for centering the film on the frame
    B. to speed up the printing process
    C. to keep the job clean
    D. to help in feeding the job

7. In making rubber stamps, mica powder is used   7.___

    A. on the vulcanizing rubber
    B. to polish the press
    C. on the molding board
    D. to prepare the stamp for mounting

8. In silk screen printing, register is obtained by   8.___

    A. pin guides   B. quad guides
    C. thumb tacks   D. paper guides

9. Photographic enlarging paper is known as _____ paper.   9.___

    A. bromide   B. chloride   C. halide   D. fluoride

10. In bookbinding, a signature is the

   A. name of the publisher
   B. author's name
   C. folded section of a book
   D. final *OK* from the customer

11. A linoleum block is a _____ printing plate.

   A. relief
   B. lithographic
   C. incised
   D. stereotype

12. A plate mark is characteristic of a print made by

   A. mitography
   B. a dry-point etching
   C. photogravure
   D. flexography

13. A hard binding should be used on a book that is

   A. edition bound
   B. hand sewn
   C. wide-wire stitched
   D. plastic bound

14. The number of 17" x 22" paper sheets needed to make 1000 pieces of 8 1/2" x 11" paper is

   A. 175
   B. 200
   C. 250
   D. 325

15. In locking a heavy form for the platen press, the form is positioned

   A. below the center of the chase
   B. according to the grippers on the press
   C. in any position sideways of the chase
   D. against the bottom of the chase

16. Proofreader's marks placed in a circle indicate the omission of a

   A. hyphen
   B. apostrophe
   C. comma
   D. period

17. Of the following, the process that is NOT used to make printing plates is _____ plate.

   A. halftone
   B. stereotype
   C. zinc
   D. lithographic

18. A line of type 4 1/2" in length will measure _____ picas.

   A. 25
   B. 26
   C. 27
   D. 28

19. Plate oil mixed with ink is used for

   A. silk screen printing
   B. lithographic printing
   C. flexographic printing
   D. printing an etching

20. Photographic contact prints are made by using a(n)

   A. printing frame
   B. enlarger
   C. vacuum frame
   D. type frame

21. Transtrace is a material used to make

   A. linoleum blocks
   B. silk screen stencils
   C. rubber stamps
   D. lithographic prints

22. The basis size of book paper is

   A. 25" x 38"
   B. 17" x 22"
   C. 22 1/2" x 28 1/2"
   D. 20" x 36"

23. The CORRECT size of professional stationery is

   A. 5 1/2" x 8 1/2"   B. 7 1/2" x 10 1/4"   C. 8 1/2" x 11"   D. 9" x 12"

24. Imposition refers to the placing of pages

   A. in the center of the chase
   B. allowing for the correct margins
   C. additional author corrections on page
   D. in correct order for folding

25. Antique finish paper is used extensively for the printing of

   A. books   B. letterheads   C. halftones   D. linecuts

KEY (CORRECT ANSWERS)

1.	C	11.	A
2.	A	12.	B
3.	D	13.	A
4.	B	14.	C
5.	A	15.	A
6.	C	16.	D
7.	A	17.	B
8.	D	18.	C
9.	A	19.	D
10.	C	20.	A

21. D
22. A
23. B
24. D
25. A

TEST 3

DIRECTIONS: Each question or incomplete statement is followed by several suggested answers or completions. Select the one that BEST answers the question or completes the statement. *PRINT THE LETTER OF THE CORRECT ANSWER IN THE SPACE AT THE RIGHT.*

1. The manufacturer's basic size for bond paper is   1.____
   A. 8 1/2" x 11"   B. 17" x 22"   C. 25" x 38"   D. 32" x 44"

2. Of the following names, the one that does NOT refer to the finish on paper is   2.____
   A. eggshell   B. antique   C. english   D. bond

3. The word *signature* refers to   3.____
   A. offset printing
   B. dry point etching
   C. book binding
   D. silk screen printing

4. The heavy starched cloth used for reinforcing the back of a book is called   4.____
   A. binder's cloth
   B. super
   C. book cloth
   D. buckram

5. Of the following, the one that is NOT a basic method of printing is   5.____
   A. relief   B. offset   C. gravure   D. silkscreen

6. The consistency of silk screen *ink* is similar to that of   6.____
   A. water
   B. paint
   C. letterpress ink
   D. job ink

7. Of the following, the one that is NOT a form of imitation engraving is   7.____
   A. lithography
   B. process embossing
   C. thermography
   D. virkotyping

8. Of the following, the one that is a part of a printing press is   8.____
   A. guides   B. packing   C. platen   D. tympan

9. To miss an impression during a run on a platen press, one uses the   9.____
   A. grippers
   B. throw-off lever
   C. chase
   D. foot treadle

10. The name *Nu-film* is related to   10.____
    A. gravure
    B. letterpress
    C. offset
    D. silk screen

11. The spacer MOST commonly used between words when setting type is   11.____
    A. em quad   B. 3-em space   C. en quad   D. 5-em space

12. To be sure a type is positioned properly in composition, one must check the   12.____
    A. feet   B. face   C. serifs   D. nicks

13. Of the following letters, the one that is NOT a *type demon* is 13.____
    A. b   B. p   C. e   D. q

14. There are 12 points in one 14.____
    A. pica   B. inch   C. nonpareil   D. lead

15. All of the following are used when locking up a form EXCEPT 15.____
    A. guides   B. quoins   C. furniture   D. chase

16. In taking proofs on a proof press, the form is held in a 16.____
    A. stick   B. case   C. galley   D. rack

17. Adjusting the impression of a printing run can BEST be accomplished by 17.____
    A. make-ready   B. moving the grippers
    C. tightening the guides   D. adjusting the platen

18. Three-color reproduction of pictures requires the use of all of the following colors EXCEPT 18.____
    A. red   B. black   C. yellow   D. blue

19. The word *slug* commonly refers to a line space of _____ points. 19.____
    A. 4   B. 2   C. 6   D. 8

20. The word *lead* commonly refers to a line space of _____ point(s). 20.____
    A. 1   B. 2   C. 3   D. 4

21. A matrix would be found on all of the following machines EXCEPT the 21.____
    A. linotype   B. Ludlow
    C. intertype   D. photocompositor

22. Of the following, the screen cut producing the CLEAREST picture would be 22.____
    A. 150   B. 100   C. 130   D. 60

23. To reproduce a photograph using the letterpress printing method, the printer would need a 23.____
    A. line cut   B. halftone
    C. line engraving D. stereotype

24. Of the following, the one that is NOT used in locking up a form is the 24.____
    A. chase   B. furniture   C. quoins   D. tympan

25. Cold-type composition is related MOST closely to _____ printing. 25.____
    A. relief   B. offset   C. italio   D. silkscreen

KEY (CORRECT ANSWERS)

1. B
2. D
3. C
4. B
5. D

6. B
7. A
8. C
9. B
10. D

11. B
12. D
13. C
14. A
15. A

16. C
17. A
18. B
19. C
20. B

21. D
22. A
23. B
24. D
25. B

TEST 4

DIRECTIONS: Each question or incomplete statement is followed by several suggested answers or completions. Select the one that BEST answers the question or completes the statement. *PRINT THE LETTER OF THE CORRECT ANSWER IN THE SPACE AT THE RIGHT.*

1. The term *side face* is used to describe one kind of 1.____

    A. bookbinding
    B. rule
    C. silk screen stencil
    D. chase

2. *Nu-film* is used in 2.____

    A. the silk screen process
    B. the Ozalid Dyphoto process
    C. the Land direct print process
    D. making offset press negatives

3. Hypo is used as a 3.____

    A. developer
    B. stop bath
    C. wetting agent
    D. fixer

4. *Work and twist* is a term used to describe a technique in 4.____

    A. printing columnar jobs
    B. printing on both sides of a sheet
    C. doping inks
    D. making certain hand-made paper

5. An example of a kerned letter is 5.____

    A. f   B. z   C. m   D. a

6. Bond inks are BEST suited for printing on 6.____

    A. rough uncoated wood fiber paper
    B. coated and enameled book stock
    C. cover stock
    D. ledger paper

7. The BEST place to add ink on the inking disc during a run on a platen press is on the _____ side. 7.____

    A. upper left
    B. upper right
    C. lower right
    D. lower left

8. The proofreader's mark *Sp. out* means 8.____

    A. remove the space
    B. space out - increase the spacing
    C. delete
    D. spell out

9. The Fourdrinier machine is used in the process of
   A. gravure printing
   B. intaglio printing
   C. paper making
   D. Tusche printing

10. Compared to *winter* rollers, *summer* ink rollers contain
    A. more glue
    B. less rubber
    C. more softening materials
    D. less glue

11. A 3-em space of 12 point type is _____ points wide.
    A. 2   B. 3   C. 4   D. 5

12. The number of 5-em spaces needed to equal a 3-em quad is
    A. 1 2/3   B. 6   C. 8   D. 15

13. Swash characters are
    A. a variation of Roman types
    B. similar to cursives
    C. special forms of some text fonts
    D. made in upper case only

14. The number of 28" x 38" sheets required for 2000 programs, 6" x 9", with a 5% allowance for spoilage, is
    A. 63   B. 66   C. 118   D. 263

15. An aniline-dye carbon paper is used in printing.
    A. offset
    B. silk screen
    C. mimeograph
    D. spirit duplicator

16. A paste-up can be reproduced on a mimeograph stencil by a
    A. scan-o-graver
    B. stenafax
    C. spirit duplicator
    D. visual duplicator

17. FREEDOM OF THE PRESS is associated with the early American printer,
    A. William Bradford
    B. Benjamin Franklin
    C. Stephen Daye
    D. John Zenger

18. A duplicate of a type form used on a letterpress is known as a(n)
    A. electrotype
    B. zinc plate
    C. halftone plate
    D. offset plate

19. If the background of a dry point etching is too dark, the cause is PROBABLY
    A. too much ink
    B. too much roller pressure
    C. inadequate wiping
    D. inadequate paper conditioning

20. In setting gauge pins on a printing press for a 3" x 5" card, the gauge pins should be placed in the following positions:
    A. One each to the left, bottom and right
    B. Two each to the left, bottom and right

C. One to the left and two at the bottom
D. Two to the left and one at the bottom

21. The inside sheets of a photo album are held together with
    A. glue
    B. wire stitches
    C. kettle stitches
    D. lacing

22. A hard binding should be used on a book that is
    A. side-wire stitched
    B. hand-sewn
    C. edition bound
    D. plastic bound

23. In printing a business card, the form is placed in the chase with the head to the
    A. left   B. bottom   C. right   D. top

24. In silk screen printing, tusche is used in making a _____ stencil.
    A. paper   B. washout   C. film   D. photographic

25. In silk screen printing, a frisket is used to
    A. center the film on the frame
    B. speed up the printing process
    C. keep the job clean
    D. help feed the job

KEY (CORRECT ANSWERS)

1. B		11. C	
2. A		12. D	
3. D		13. B	
4. A		14. C	
5. A		15. D	
6. D		16. B	
7. D		17. D	
8. D		18. A	
9. C		19. C	
10. A		20. C	

21. D
22. C
23. B
24. B
25. C

EXAMINATION SECTION
TEST 1

DIRECTIONS: Each question or incomplete statement is followed by several suggested answers or completions. Select the one that BEST answers the question or completes the statement. *PRINT THE LETTER OF THE CORRECT ANSWER IN THE SPACE AT THE RIGHT.*

1. Which of the following is a nonsilver coating for photographic contact printing?

    A. Intaglio   B. Mezzotint   C. Cicero   D. Diazo

2. According to the *sequence* principle in design, the eye usually travels in each of the following ways when viewing a printed page EXCEPT from

    A. the upper-left corner to the lower-right
    B. big to small
    C. black to color
    D. bold to light

3. If any part of the image area on the plate deteriorates during the printing process, _____ has occurred.

    A. slurring   B. warp
    C. calendering   D. walk-off

4. Kneaded rubber erasers are most appropriate for use with

    A. chalks and charcoals   B. pencil
    C. drawing ink   D. dirt

5. In printing, any copy suitable for reproduction without using a halftone screen is referred to as _____ copy.

    A. hot   B. wireframe   C. line   D. hard

6. Which of the following steps in preparing a mechanical is typically performed LAST?

    A. Marking bleed lines   B. Pasting down type and art
    C. Marking key lines   D. Preparing an overlay

7. Which of the following is a typical bit depth for grayscale images in computer applications?

    A. 1   B. 8   C. 14   D. 24

8. Which of the following characteristics of color is used to describe lightness or darkness?

    A. Chroma   B. Saturation
    C. Hue   D. Value

9. A general rule in design is that if reverse print is used, it should not be set in type smaller than _____ points, in order to be readable.

    A. 10   B. 12   C. 14   D. 18

10. In print technology, the simulation of tones by using dot patterns of varying intensity is known as

    A. halftoning
    B. stippling
    C. grayscaling
    D. pixellation

11. Which of the following is NOT a rule of thumb for the capitalization of headlines during mechanical preparation?

    A. Capitalize any word with four or more letters.
    B. The most readable headlines are written in all caps.
    C. As an infinitive, *To* is always capitalized, but not as a preposition.
    D. Any word that starts a line should be capitalized, even if it is in the middle of the headline.

12. In CAD/CAM applications, what is the term for the feature which tells the user where he or she is in terms of the x, y, or z coordinates?

    A. Coordinate tracking
    B. Virtual reality
    C. User-defined views
    D. Auto-dimensioning

13. Which of the following is the most appropriate use for hot-press illustration board?

    A. Layouts
    B. First roughs
    C. Transferring sketches
    D. Mechanicals

14. Which of the following processes is involved in the preparation of a *flat* for offset printing plate exposure?

    A. Keylining
    B. Trapping
    C. Stripping
    D. Markup

15. In typography, how many points make up a pica?

    A. 6
    B. 9
    C. 12
    D. 18

16. Each of the following is a common benefit associated with the use of a mechanical in the preparation of artwork for press EXCEPT it

    A. saves time
    B. assures proper positioning of images on the page
    C. keeps type and line art elements intact as one unit
    D. allows proofing of in-place elements at a stage in production where changes are inexpensive

17. During color separation, a blue filter

    A. reflects yellow and cyan onto film
    B. absorbs all colors to create a black printer
    C. leaves nearly transparent areas in the cyan portions of the image
    D. leaves nearly transparent areas in the yellow portions of the image

18. Digital printing is fostering several essentially new printing markets that have not been prevalent in the past due to the cost of prepress and printing by conventional methods. Which of the following is NOT one of these markets?
    _____ printing.

    A. On-demand
    B. Batch-processed
    C. Short-run process
    D. Variable information

19. Each of the following statements about artist's drawing ink is true EXCEPT they
    A. are an excellent medium for line drawing
    B. are not transparent
    C. have good adhesion properties
    D. are waterproof

20. To offset the different ink layers in conventional process color separations, halftone screens for black should be placed at a _____° angle to one another to avoid undesirable moire patterns.
    A. 45 B. 75 C. 90 D. 105

21. Letterpress
    A. runs tend to be inconsistent
    B. does not have good halftone detail
    C. offers excellent tints
    D. is especially suited to textured paper

22. The LEAST expensive printing surfaces available today are
    A. intaglio plates
    B. thermal serial heads
    C. lithographic plates
    D. gravure rollers

23. Orange or red transparent masking film is typically used to
    A. define the trim marks on a mechanical
    B. define an area to be screened or tinted
    C. define a knockout
    D. prevent bleeding during the printing process

24. Each of the following is a component of the Agfa Chroma-press system for color printing EXCEPT
    A. RIP or raster image processor
    B. job entry subsystem
    C. output print engine
    D. server software

25. During paste-up, windows for halftones that are intended to bleed into the margin should be _____ in. beyond the trin line.
    A. 1/16 to 1/8
    B. 1/8 to 1/4
    C. 1/4 to 1/2
    D. 1/2 to 1

KEY (CORRECT ANSWERS)

1. D
2. C
3. D
4. A
5. C

6. D
7. B
8. D
9. A
10. A

11. B
12. A
13. D
14. C
15. C

16. A
17. D
18. B
19. B
20. A

21. C
22. C
23. B
24. B
25. B

———

TEST 2

DIRECTIONS: Each question or incomplete statement is followed by several suggested answers or completions. Select the one that BEST answers the question or completes the statement. *PRINT THE LETTER OF THE CORRECT ANSWER IN THE SPACE AT THE RIGHT.*

1. To secure all elements in place during the preparation of a mechanical, each of the following tools may be used EXCEPT 1._____

   A. a burnishing roller
   B. opaquing liquid
   C. smooth ivory stick
   D. a burnishing stick

2. Adjustable triangles used in design work should at the very least be _____ inches long on one side. 2._____

   A. 6 B. 8 C. 10 D. 14

3. The flat or rolled surface against which paper is held during the printing process is generally known as the 3._____

   A. raster
   B. litho plate
   C. platen
   D. blanket cylinder

4. Which of the following is an *oldstyle* typeface? 4._____

   A. Folio B. Times C. Helvetica D. Garamond

5. During the preparation of a mechanical, the image area should be positioned so that at LEAST a _____-inch margin exists outside of it for the placement of registration and other marks. 5._____

   A. $\frac{1}{2}$ B. 1 C. $1\frac{1}{2}$ D. 2

6. During color separation, an artist might prepare copy by outlining certain areas of the artwork on a tissue overlay, with instructions to the printer or camera operator. This is a process known as 6._____

   A. cropping B. keylining C. stripping D. keystoning

7. Which of the following is a common use for a torchon in artwork? 7._____

   A. Bisecting a drawn line
   B. Achieving a fine point on a drawing pencil
   C. Masking off areas on the drawing surface
   D. Blending charcoal particles on the drawing surface

8. Which of the following is a form of proof from stripped film flats that is made before final plates are burned, in order to ensure correct pagination and location of illustrations and photos? 8._____

   A. Brownout
   B. Master proof
   C. Blueline
   D. Color proof

49

9. When working with a photograph during paste-up, an artist finds that the image is gray and flat in overall appearance. Which of the following is the best solution for improving a reprint?

    A. Use the burning-in technique
    B. Use the dodging technique
    C. Reproduce the shot as small as possible
    D. Trying a duller finish on the print

10. _____ is the prepress technique which allows for slight variations in registration during the press run.

    A. Trapping   B. Dithering
    C. Antialiasing   D. Stripping

11. Usually, holding lines on a mechanical are drawn in

    A. nonrepro blue pencil
    B. red ink with a ruling or technical pen
    C. cobalt blue ink with a ruling or technical pen
    D. black with a ruling or technical pen

12. When the action of light through positives produces a light-hardened coating on the non-image areas of lithographic printing plates, the plates are described as

    A. lossy   B. negative   C. halftoned   D. deep-etched

13. In computer graphics, a curve calculated by a mathematical function that connects separate points with a high degree of smoothness is known specifically as a(n)

    A. sine   B. Bezier   C. rollout   D. spline

14. What is the term for a line that extends from the outside edge of an object being dimensioned out to where the dimension text is printed?

    A. Witness line   B. Frontis
    C. Vector   D. Wireframe

15. In composing thumbnails, an artist should be concerned with each of the following EXCEPT

    A. shade   B. proportion
    C. weight   D. scale

16. Which of the following is a type of optical device used in the art studio to project enlarged or reduced images for tracing?

    A. Histogram   B. Lucey   C. Extruder   D. Overset

17. Which of the following brush types include short, curved-in, flat brushes?

    A. Flats   B. Brights   C. Fans   D. Sky

18. Which of the following is LEAST likely to be a problem associated with electrophotographic printing?
    A. There may be variations in batches of toners with identical formulations.
    B. There is currently no means of smoothing bitmapped screen fonts or images during printing.
    C. Volatile organic compounds used in liquid toner systems are subject to environmental regulations.
    D. Image density and tone reproduction may suffer as a result of charge voltage decay.

19. An item of artwork is to be reduced on a mechanical so that its width of 40 picas becomes a finished width of 10 picas. Assuming that the reduction is proportional, what percentage reduction will be necessary to achieve the finished width?
    A. 25   B. 33   C. 75   D. 400

20. Which of the following shading techniques in image processing renders facets of a polygon model as a single color based on their orientation to light and the viewer?
    A. Phong   B. Gouraud   C. Smooth   D. Flat

21. Which of the following is most suitable for transferring sketches to final art?
    A. Hot-press illustration board
    B. Bond paper
    C. Multi-media vellum
    D. Kid-finish bristol

22. What is the term for a calculation that determines how much space copy will take up when it is typeset?
    A. Assembly   B. Pulse   C. Spike   D. Castoff

23. When inking in stencils during layouts, the pen should generally be held at a _____° angle to the paper in order to ensure accuracy.
    A. 45   B. 60   C. 75   D. 90

24. To avoid trapping in a print job, one can create colors by overprinting, but in order for this to work there must be at LEAST _____% commonality in the colors placed adjacent to each other.
    A. 10   B. 20   C. 35   D. 50

25. In page printing, the folded sets of pages produced are known as
    A. signatures   B. impositions
    C. scores   D. flats

KEY (CORRECT ANSWERS)

1. B
2. C
3. C
4. D
5. B

6. B
7. D
8. C
9. D
10. A

11. B
12. D
13. D
14. A
15. C

16. B
17. B
18. B
19. C
20. D

21. C
22. D
23. D
24. B
25. A

EXAMINATION SECTION
TEST 1

DIRECTIONS: Each question or incomplete statement is followed by several suggested answers or completions. Select the one that BEST answers the question or completes the statement. *PRINT THE LETTER OF THE CORRECT ANSWER IN THE SPACE AT THE RIGHT.*

1. Which of the following is a type of color proof that represents the process combinations to be printed from four-color film?

    A. Pantone   B. Color Key   C. Lucey   D. Chromalin

2. In digital printing, _____ is the term used to denote pronounceable delineations between color and shading gradations.

    A. aliasing   B. banding   C. lapping   D. feathering

3. What is the term for the type of layout that features a single large illustration that dominates the space?

    A. Omnibus
    B. Silhouette
    C. Picture window
    D. Knockout

4. Which of the following characters has a unit count of 1½?

    A. L   B. ?   C. F   D. Y

5. The main difference between constructing a halftone window and making a screen or tint is that

    A. a screen is attached at the top with masking tape
    B. the window is on an overlay
    C. a screen can be supplied by the printer at the time press plates are made
    D. the window is on the basic artwork

6. To avoid *banding* in a scanned color image, an artist should have enough steps in the blend so that the length of each step is _____ points or less.

    A. 2   B. 4   C. 6   D. 8

7. Which of the following is used as a masking film to cover large image areas on mechanicals?

    A. Clear acetate
    B. Prepared acetate
    C. Amberlith
    D. Rubylith

8. Which of the following is NOT a disadvantage associated with the use of drum-based imagesetters for printing?

    A. Waste of film and time
    B. Limited imaging area
    C. Low-quality output
    D. High cost

9. Which of the following is a serif typeface?

    A. Myriad
    B. Avant Garde
    C. Century Schoolbook
    D. Helvetica

10. Rather than photographing each piece of art or photography separately for shooting negatives, they can be grouped together in a process known as

    A. clumping   B. clogging   C. chaining   D. ganging

11. If *FPO* is found written on a mechanical, it means that

    A. the proofreader has examined and approved the original copy
    B. there has been an error made by the printer or the typesetter
    C. the color on a prepress proof needs to be corrected
    D. the sized copy of a photograph or illustration is not to be used as camera-ready art

12. In which of the following types of presses are white highlights impossible?

    A. Flexography
    B. Duplicate offset
    C. Screen
    D. Xerography

13. During the printing process, which of the following is placed in direct contact with film in order to screen halftones?

    A. Line screen
    B. Platen
    C. Splitter
    D. Contact screen

14. Which of the following drawing media is most likely to produce a muddy, overworked effect in artwork?

    A. Fabricated chalk
    B. Oil pastel
    C. Crayon
    D. Charcoal

15. During the preparation of a mechanical, which of the following is the easiest way to lengthen copy that has already been set?

    A. Cutting text apart between paragraphs and adding more space
    B. Allowing more space between letters
    C. Setting paragraphs fully flush to the margins
    D. Add leading between lines

16. Printing paper that measures 20" x 25" is referred to specifically as

    A. board   B. bond   C. rule   D. royal

17. Which of the following is a possible DISADVANTAGE associated with the use of fm screening applications over halftone screening for the reproduction of tones in an image?

    A. Greater necessity for overprinting
    B. Lower ink densities reduce tonal range and contrast
    C. Ratio of white area to inked area changes can alter transfer curve calculations
    D. Larger printing dots create lower image detail

18. When a printed image is described as *low key*, it means it

    A. does not use halftones
    B. appears on the bottom half of the page
    C. takes up less than 1/4 of the page or surface
    D. is composed primarily of dark tones

19. On a printing press, the rubber-covered cylinders that transfer ink from the fountain onto the ink drum are known as the

    A. jack rollers
    B. distributing rollers
    C. impression cylinders
    D. blanket cylinders

20. During paste-up of copy, the rule of thumb is to typeset at least _____ to correct a single word or letter, so that the correction can be aligned properly.

    A. three words of type
    B. one line of type
    C. two lines of type
    D. the entire paragraph

21. What is the term for a printing press that prints both sides of the paper at one pass through the machine?

    A. Perfector
    B. Pointer
    C. Slug
    D. Web press

22. When using colored pastels for artwork, a solution of _____, worked in with a small brush, can help to spread the color evenly over the surface.

    A. water
    B. washing soda
    C. paint thinner
    D. white gouache

23. Which of the following is a term for the degree to which a paper changes shape as a result of a change in atmospheric relative humidity?

    A. Distortion
    B. Expansivity
    C. Elongation
    D. Rigidity

24. An advantage of a duotone design over a duograph is that it

    A. counts as two colors for budgeting and scheduling purposes
    B. adds a second color by using an area of light color
    C. retains shadows and highlights
    D. uses only one negative

25. Which of the following is typically drawn first in the preparation of a mechanical?

    A. Bleed lines
    B. Crop marks
    C. Fold lines
    D. Outline

KEY (CORRECT ANSWERS)

1.	D	11.	D
2.	B	12.	A
3.	C	13.	D
4.	D	14.	B
5.	D	15.	A
6.	A	16.	D
7.	C	17.	C
8.	C	18.	D
9.	C	19.	B
10.	D	20.	C

21. A
22. C
23. B
24. C
25. D

TEST 2

DIRECTIONS: Each question or incomplete statement is followed by several suggested answers or completions. Select the one that BEST answers the question or completes the statement. *PRINT THE LETTER OF THE CORRECT ANSWER IN THE SPACE AT THE RIGHT.*

1. When ruling paste-up sheets that include camera-ready artwork for printing, vertical center lines and top trim lines should be drawn in
    I. pencil
    II. black ink
    III. nonrepro blue ink
   The CORRECT answer is:

   A. I only   B. II only   C. I or III   D. I, II, or III

   1.____

2. The process of reducing the size of a knockout when colors overlap one another is known as

   A. choking   B. chopping
   C. cropping   D. chromaticizing

   2.____

3. Which of the following is most suitable for making carbon and photocopies?

   A. Fine line marker   B. Technical pen
   C. Mechanical pencil   D. Rolling writer

   3.____

4. In lithographic press work, *hickeys* are likely to be caused by each of the following EXCEPT

   A. dry, hard particles on the printing plate or blanket
   B. hardened specks of ink
   C. an out-of-round transfer roller
   D. dirt on the press

   4.____

5. Which of the following groups of typefaces makes use of the most radical *thick/thin* transition?

   A. Sans serif   B. Modern
   C. Slab serif   D. Oldstyle

   5.____

6. Whenever an overlay is to be used during paste-up without pin registration, at least _____ transfer registration marks should be used on at least two sides of the basic artwork for alignment with corresponding marks on the overlay?

   A. 2   B. 3   C. 5   D. 6

   6.____

7. Which of the following is/are advantages of indirect color separation over direct color separation?
    I. Faster and more efficient
    II. Greater control over color quality of the final negatives
    III. Allows for making different-sized separations from the intermediate steps without having to repeat the first part of the process
   The CORRECT answer is:

   A. I only   B. I, II   C. II, III   D. III only

   7.____

8. Which element of an electrophotographic imaging system is used to clean the photoconductor of the image just printed?

   A. Corona
   B. Photoreceptor belt
   C. Drum
   D. Solvent

9. Each of the following means the same as *degeneration* when working with art EXCEPT

   A. tone line conversion
   B. linear definition
   C. posterization
   D. two-tone posterization

10. In process-color reproduction, the process of masking is used primarily to

    A. select a portion of an image by cutting away parts from its edges
    B. electronically capture a single picture element
    C. reduce the size of a knockout when colors overlap
    D. reduce the contrast of transmitted light

11. In typography, how many picas make up an inch of type?

    A. 6   B. 10   C. 12   D. 14

12. In computer graphics, what is the term for a visible defect in an image that is typically caused by limitations in the input or output processes?

    A. Artifact   B. Spike   C. Bit error   D. Alias

13. Which of the following types or proofs are made of photosensitive paper that has been exposed with plate negatives?

    A. Pre-press proofs
    B. Press proofs
    C. Progressive proofs
    D. Blues

14. Which of the following progressive color proofs would be presented FIRST before the production run?

    A. Blue plate alone
    B. Black alone
    C. Yellow alone
    D. Yellow, red, and blue

15. In design, *balance* describes a state of equilibrium in which visual forces of equal strength pull in opposite directions. Which of the following is not a type of balance used in design work?

    A. Symmetrical
    B. Asymmetrical
    C. Centrifugal
    D. Radial

16. Which of the following is a printing method in which the image area is etched below the surface of the printing plate?

    A. Diazo
    B. Lithography
    C. Gravure
    D. Flexography

17. When an area of a photograph is too dark to reproduce well, the process of _____ may lighten it.

    A. dodging
    B. vignetting
    C. burning-in
    D. time exposure

18. A ream of paper in a print shop is labeled as *extensible*.
    This means that the paper

    A. can expand and contract with humidity and still hold an image
    B. is only to be used for electrostatic printing
    C. will withstand a sudden shock without tearing
    D. can be printed on both sides

19. Which of the following is LEAST likely to be a cause of press misregistration during the printing process?

    A. Plate misalignment
    B. Changes in humidity
    C. Changes in temperature
    D. High-speed paper handling

20. Which of the following is considered good design practice in typography?

    A. Choose a typeface that is short and thick to offset a tall and slender typeface
    B. Use a script and an italic on the same page
    C. Add importance to one element by making it bolder, and to another on the same page by making it bigger
    D. Using two scripts on the same page

21. Which of the following is an abbreviation for the chemical used to remove undeveloped silver from the emulsion of photographic film?

    A. Repro   B. Chroma   C. Hypo   D. Lucey

22. When ruling dummy sheets for a mechanical, which of the following may be ruled in picas, rather than inches or centimeters?

    A. Art measures   B. Gutters
    C. Spaces between columns   D. Margins

23. Photostats that are line converted are known as

    A. veloxes   B. luceys
    C. master stats   D. halftones

24. In CAD/CAM applications, users can determine the physical characteristics of a given object by making use of a feature known as

    A. auto-dimensioning   B. solids modeling
    C. layering   D. user-defined views

25. Which of the following devices is used to determine correct photographic exposure for consistency on press?

    A. Lucey   B. Halftone screen
    C. Densitometer D. Equalizer

KEY (CORRECT ANSWERS)

1. B
2. A
3. D
4. C
5. B

6. B
7. C
8. A
9. C
10. D

11. A
12. A
13. D
14. C
15. C

16. C
17. A
18. C
19. C
20. A

21. C
22. A
23. A
24. B
25. C

EXAMINATION SECTION
TEST 1

DIRECTIONS: Each question or incomplete statement is followed by several suggested answers or completions. Select the one that BEST answers the question or completes the statement. *PRINT THE LETTER OF THE CORRECT ANSWER IN THE SPACE AT THE RIGHT.*

1. Finished art and mechanicals are typically based on the 1.____
   - A. thumbnail
   - B. rough layout
   - C. color proof
   - D. rough comprehensive

2. Which of the following is a DISADVANTAGE associated with the use of offset printing rather than letterpress or gravure? 2.____
   - A. Usually a slower process overall
   - B. More limited in the type of layouts that can be used
   - C. Less accommodating of reverses
   - D. Less intense inking

3. Instructions for a printing job that include the correct page sequence, an identification of all unnumbered pages, layout specifications, and strip-in instructions are gathered collectively on the 3.____
   - A. master list
   - B. assembly sheet
   - C. composite
   - D. balance sheet

4. In Tag Image File Format (TIFF), a pixel is represented by a single bit in 4.____
   - A. a monochrome picture
   - B. binary line art
   - C. a binary picture
   - D. a grayscale

5. In color printing, an undesirable pattern may occur when reproductions are made from halftones, especially if screens are misaligned or at an improper angle. What is the term for this result? 5.____
   - A. Moiré
   - B. Hickey
   - C. Ghosting
   - D. Slurring

6. Which of the following drawing instruments is most appropriate for hand-lettering design? 6.____
   - A. Hard-lead mechanical pencil
   - B. #2 pencil
   - C. Razor-point felt-tipped pen
   - D. Hardmuth pencil

7. Which of the following press types is best for non-paper surfaces? 7.____
   - A. Gravure
   - B. Duplicator offset
   - C. Quality offset
   - D. Screen

8. Which of the following types of finished art is generally preferred because it yields better contrasts for reproduction? 8.____
   - A. Black-and-white print
   - B. Color print
   - C. Transparency
   - D. Color negative

9. If pure, saturated colors are desired as an output, which of the following color correction methods is most appropriate? _____ rendering.

   A. Solid color
   B. Photographic
   C. Presentation graphics
   D. Perceptual

10. The rectangular metal frame in which hot metal type and plates are positioned and locked up for letterpress printing is known as the

    A. platen   B. chase   C. quoin   D. choke

11. Which of the following is used to explain what is presented in a graph, chart, diagram, map, or other technical illustration?

    A. Caption   B. Legend   C. Slug line   D. Cutline

12. What is the printing term for a group of camera-ready layout elements mounted and ready for photographing?

    A. Signature
    B. Composition
    C. Flat
    D. Chain

13. In lithographic platemaking, the process of _____ makes nonimage areas of the plate nonreceptive to ink.

    A. desensitization
    B. etching
    C. stripping
    D. filtering

14. Positioning _____ is typically the first stage in preparing a mechanical dummy for paste-up.

    A. line art
    B. text type
    C. graphics and photography
    D. non-text type

15. Which of the following is a general rule for the design of artwork?

    A. Photographs or illustrations should be positioned so that they face outward from within a page or spread.
    B. Photographs or illustrations with a common horizon should be placed slightly out of alignment.
    C. A *heavy* shot becomes darker as it becomes larger.
    D. Art that is heavy because of bulk or dark tones should be placed low on the page.

16. When a printing press fails to reproduce dots — that is, when no dots are visible — the mechanism is described as

    A. clogged
    B. calendered
    C. plugged
    D. caked

17. When pasting up mechanical artwork for gravure printing, each of the following is a guideline or rule EXCEPT

    A. all elements on the mechanical must be able to tolerate a halftone screen
    B. only one-piece mechanicals can be used for printing
    C. all line work should be included on the basic artwork
    D. transfer shading films should not be used

18. To accomplish quality color printing, accurate positioning of two or more colors of ink is required. This is referred to as

    A. spread B. register C. grip D. lap

19. For each of the following media in an airbrush, it is necessary to use a pressure of 40-50 pounds per square inch (psi) EXCEPT

    A. acrylics B. dyes C. lacquers D. enamels

20. The halftone window of a mechanical is to have a narrow, even margin of white around it to stand out on a screened page. The engraver on the print job will probably prefer that the window be made

    A. by ruling the space in black ink, using no masking film
    B. by using orange or red transparent masking film, taped onto an acetate overlay
    C. with a keyline, drawing the image area on a tissue-paper overlay
    D. by using orange or red transparent masking film, burnished onto the mechanical

21. If one wants to avoid the paste-up stage entirely, which of the following methods should be used to prepare type or graphics for output?

    A. Antialiasing B. Area composition
    C. Imposition D. Cropping

22. As a general rule, paper to be die-cut should be of at least a _____-lb. bond or heavier as the design to be die-cut increases in detail.

    A. 10 B. 20 C. 30 D. 40

23. Because of the difficulties associated with its use, _____ should be avoided if possible when adding rules and borders to a mechanical.

    A. a ruling pen B. transfer art
    C. a typeset line D. a typeset leader

24. Each of the following is an appropriate use for fine-line markers EXCEPT

    A. accomplishing precise roughs and layouts
    B. rendering small type
    C. marking fold lines
    D. sketching

25. What term is used to describe photographic surfaces which are insensitive to red, but sensitive to ultraviolet, blue, green, yellow, and orange rays?

    A. Polychromatic B. Panchromatic
    C. Apochromatic D. Orthochromatic

KEY (CORRECT ANSWERS)

1. D
2. D
3. B
4. C
5. A

6. D
7. D
8. C
9. C
10. B

11. B
12. C
13. A
14. B
15. D

16. C
17. B
18. B
19. B
20. A

21. B
22. B
23. A
24. C
25. D

TEST 2

DIRECTIONS: Each question or incomplete statement is followed by several suggested answers or completions. Select the one that BEST answers the question or completes the statement. *PRINT THE LETTER OF THE CORRECT ANSWER IN THE SPACE AT THE RIGHT.*

1. Which of the following is/are disadvantages associated with the use of clear acetate for overlays?
    I. Does not hold liquid media well
    II. Often becomes discolored with use
    III. May stretch or shrink with temperature
   The CORRECT answer is:

   A. I, II
   B. I, III
   C. II, III
   D. None of the above

2. The main DISADVANTAGE associated with the use of overlays during the preparation of a mechanical is that they

   A. do not mask out areas according to color
   B. may add time later to the process of color separation
   C. may not produce a register that is acceptably close
   D. cannot be used to specify halftones

3. Which of the following characteristics of color is used to describe brightness or dullness?

   A. Saturation
   B. Tone
   C. Hue
   D. Value

4. When working with light sensitive plate coatings, which of the following are most likely to produce a dark reaction? High
    I. humidity
    II. pressure
    III. temperature
   The CORRECT answer is:

   A. I only   B. I, II   C. I, III   D. I, II, III

5. What is the term for the type of layout that uses a combination of rectangles (usually illustrations) placed close together?

   A. Mondrian
   B. Omnibus
   C. Copy-heavy
   D. Type-specimen

6. When using a letterpress, what is the protective paper used to cover any part of a printing plate not meant to print?

   A. Crop   B. Frisket   C. Choker   D. Flap

7. In commercial printing applications, halftone screens of between _____ lines/inch are most commonly used.

   A. 50-112   B. 120-166   C. 177-220   D. 245-300

8. When burnishing elements in place during the preparation of a mechanical, one should work from

   A. left to right
   B. the center outward
   C. the margins inward
   D. the top down

9. For practical purposes, T-squares used on drawing tables should ideally be

   A. made of wood
   B. made of plastic
   C. made of stainless steel
   D. built into the table

10. In most printing processes using cylinders, the inked plate transfers the image to the paper via the _____ cylinder, which is covered with a rubber sheet.

    A. litho
    B. plate
    C. impression
    D. blanket

11. The most exact way of showing what a final printed product will look like is to compose a(n)

    A. presentation comprehensive
    B. overlay
    C. tight comprehensive
    D. rough layout

12. Which of the following is an inking instrument that is used to compare dimensions or proportions?

    A. Drawing compass
    B. Divider
    C. Ruling pen
    D. Technical pen

13. Which of the following groups of typefaces is also known as Clarendon?

    A. Script
    B. Oldstyle
    C. Sans serif
    D. Slab serif

14. In computer graphics applications, the technique of _____ can be used to simulate gradations of gray by using dot patterns.

    A. aliasing
    B. feathering
    C. dithering
    D. dot etching

15. An artist plans to use Castell 9000 pencils for matt drafting film. Typically, what grades are most appropriate for use in this application?

    A. 8B to IB   B. 8B to 3H   C. 4B to 5H   D. HB to 6H

16. In the print shop, a paper is sometimes run between polished steel rolls to give it desired smoothness. This process is known as

    A. calendering
    B. sizing
    C. caking
    D. slurring

17. To offset the different ink layers in conventional process color separations, halftone screens for yellow should be placed at a _____° angle to one another to avoid undesirable moire patterns.

    A. 45   B. 75   C. 90   D. 105

18. Which of the following would NOT be used as an overprint color?

    A. Green B. Yellow C. Red D. Blue

19. During color separation, a red filter

    A. leaves magenta areas of the image transparent
    B. reflects cyan and magenta onto film
    C. leaves cyan areas of the film transparent
    D. reflects yellow and cyan onto film

20. When preparing a mechanical, it is important to remember that the typical gripper margin to be allowed is usually _____ inch, probably at the top or bottom of the sheet.

    A. 1/4 B. 1/2 C. 1 D. $1\frac{1}{2}$

21. In the rough layout phase of art preparation, the artist should pay close attention to

    A. trapping
    B. color separation
    C. the weight and size of characters
    D. the photographic art to be used

22. What is the term for a process in which an image is pressed down into the paper surface?

    A. Engraving B. Debossing
    C. Embossing D. Lithography

23. In design, fine-point ball-point pens are most useful for

    A. mechanical indications for trim, crop, or bleed
    B. trapping
    C. sketching and rendering
    D. drawing dimensions on mechanicals

24. When preparing a mechanical, which of the following may be used to draw guidelines?
    I. Pencil
    II. Black ink
    III. Nonrepro blue ink
    The CORRECT answer is:

    A. I *only* B. I or II
    C. II or III D. I, II or III

25. Whatever kind of mechanical pencil is chosen for artwork, the lead guard should measure at LEAST _____ long at its shortest point if it is to be used with stencils.

    A. 0.2 B. 1.75 C. 3.5 D. 5

KEY (CORRECT ANSWERS)

1. B
2. C
3. A
4. C
5. A

6. B
7. B
8. B
9. C
10. D

11. A
12. B
13. D
14. C
15. D

16. A
17. C
18. B
19. C
20. B

21. C
22. B
23. A
24. C
25. C

EXAMINATION SECTION
TEST 1

DIRECTIONS: Each question or incomplete statement is followed by several suggested answers or completions. Select the one that BEST answers the question or completes the statement. *PRINT THE LETTER OF THE CORRECT ANSWER IN THE SPACE AT THE RIGHT.*

1. What is the term for the minimum pressure at which proper ink transfer is possible on a press?   1._____

    A. Push-lock
    C. Kiss pressure
    B. Doctor pressure
    D. Pickup point

2. Which of the following measuring instruments is equipped with both point and 1/64" increments?   2._____

    A. Proportion wheel
    C. Ellipse template
    B. Haberule line gauge
    D. Schaedler precision rule

3. Each of the following is an advantage associated with the use of drop-on-demand inkjet printing over continuous inkjet printing EXCEPT   3._____

    A. more compact size
    C. quieter operation
    B. higher resolution
    D. lower cost

4. Which of the following types of erasers is most appropriate for removing ink and dirt from artwork?   4._____

    A. Plastic
    C. Pink Pearl
    B. Artgum
    D. Kneaded rubber

5. On high quality projects, which of the following would most likely not be used as an adhesive during paste-up?   5._____

    A. Spray adhesive
    C. Clear tape
    B. Rubber cement
    D. Hot wax

6. Which of the following is the best material for pasting up negative art?   6._____

    A. Kid-finish bristol
    B. Bond paper
    C. Black construction paper
    D. Prepared acetate

7. Which of the following materials may be used to form the printing image base on a bimetal printing plate?   7._____

    A. Chromium
    C. Stainless steel
    B. Copper
    D. Aluminum

8. Which of the following is most appropriate for use with stencils?   8._____

    A. Fine line marker
    C. Drafting pen
    B. Layout marker
    D. Rolling writer

9. To offset the different ink layers in conventional process color separations, halftone screens for cyan should be placed at a _____° angle to one another to avoid undesirable moiré patterns.

   A. 45 B. 75 C. 90 D. 105

10. Which of the following is most appropriate for ruling mechanicals?

    A. Technical pen
    B. Divider
    C. Razor-point felt-tipped pen
    D. Non-repro blue pencil

11. Which of the following brush types include oval-shaped, full brushes that are good for laying broad washes?

    A. Fans B. Sky C. Flats D. Brights

12. Which of the following color conversion methods is most effective for spot colors, and maintains an absolute color match?
    _____ rendering.

    A. Solid color
    B. Photographic
    C. Perceptual
    D. Presentation graphics

13. For most applications, the width-to-height ratio for layouts most commonly used is

    A. 1:2 B. 2:3 C. 3:5 D. 1:4

14. Even though dummies are made in numerical or reading sequence, the mechanical of paginated work should probably be done in imposition, so that

    A. allowance is made for *creep* or shingling
    B. facing pages can be visualized together
    C. paste-up is not needlessly slowed
    D. pages will be in order when the signature is ordered and bound

15. In designing artwork and copy for a printed page or board, which of the following ratios of artwork or photography to type is considered the *golden mean*?

    A. 1 to 1 B. 1 to 2 C. 3 to 5 D. 1 to 4

16. Each of the following is an important advantage associated with press proofs EXCEPT

    A. they are made with the actual inks and paper to be used on the job
    B. they can be made quickly and inexpensively
    C. progressive proofs and proof books can be made
    D. multiple proofs can be produced at a reasonable cost

17. Which of the following statements about quality offset printing is FALSE?
    It

    A. is especially suited to textured paper
    B. is better for flat color reproduction than process color reproduction
    C. offers excellent halftone detail
    D. is generally considered to be the most economic for quality in quantity

18. Digital printing may be used to render an image in which the vertical dimension of the presentation is smaller than the horizontal dimension. This practice is known as

    A. latent-image perspective
    B. landscape orientation
    C. portrait orientation
    D. vanishing-point perspective

19. Which of the following are advantages associated with converting a halftone to a line negative during print making?
    I. Allows full assembly of a piece on the mechanical
    II. Improves image quality
    III. Saves engraver time

    The CORRECT answer is:

    A. I *only*
    B. I, III
    C. II, III
    D. None of the above

20. Which of the following is a term for the nonprintable area of a print plate?

    A. Layback
    B. Buffer
    C. Gripper margin
    D. Frame

21. The blades used with X-acto knives during mechanical preparation and paste-up are most commonly

    A. #5 and #9
    B. #8 and #10
    C. #11 and #16
    D. #12 and #18

22. Which of the following processes can produce a realistic 2-D image from a 3-D object formation?

    A. Extrusion
    B. Retrenching
    C. Rendering
    D. Extension

23. Which of the following media can be used to produce either line or continuous-tone art?

    A. Marker
    B. Scratchboard
    C. Ink wash
    D. Charcoal

24. In computer graphics, the display space border beyond which graphics display is blanked is known as the

    A. crop margin
    B. ivory board
    C. clip boundary
    D. skip tag

25. What type of mechanical pencil lead is most suitable for use on plastic drafting film?

    A. Graphite
    B. Plastic polymer-based
    C. Simple polymer-based
    D. Oiled graphite

KEY (CORRECT ANSWERS)

1. C
2. D
3. B
4. A
5. C

6. C
7. B
8. C
9. D
10. A

11. B
12. A
13. B
14. D
15. C

16. B
17. B
18. B
19. B
20. A

21. C
22. C
23. D
24. C
25. B

TEST 2

DIRECTIONS: Each question or incomplete statement is followed by several suggested answers or completions. Select the one that BEST answers the question or completes the statement. *PRINT THE LETTER OF THE CORRECT ANSWER IN THE SPACE AT THE RIGHT.*

1. Which of the following factors involved in the misregistration of ink in a printed image is most specific to digital applications?

    A. Inaccurate imagesetter generating color separation
    B. Unstable film or stripping material
    C. Platemaking errors
    D. Lack of proper environmental controls

    1.____

2. Typically, _____ typefaces all use diagonal stress.

    A. sans serif   B. script
    C. modern   D. oldstyle

    2.____

3. In computer graphics, the technique of creating a 3-D shape by stretching a 2-D shape along a third axis is known as

    A. solids modeling   B. wireframe modeling
    C. Bézier curving   D. extrusion

    3.____

4. Concerning gouache, which of the following statements is FALSE?

    A. Colors look lighter dry then wet.
    B. It has smoother flow than watercolor.
    C. It is a transparent medium.
    D. High-quality gouache can be used in a pen or airbrush.

    4.____

5. An item of artwork is to be reduced on a mechanical so that its width of 80 picas becomes a finished width of 20 picas. If the reduced image is to be proportional, and the depth of the image is 120 picas, how many picas will the finished depth of the image be?

    A. 15   B. 30   C. 45   D. 60

    5.____

6. The main DISADVANTAGE associated with the use of bitmapped fonts in computer-generated copy is that they

    A. do not scale up and down in size very well
    B. do not permit the use of sans serif fonts
    C. prevent the use of dingbats or symbols
    D. involve the use of complicated algorithms

    6.____

7. A project with _____ color register has two or more opaque colors that don't print closer than 1/16 inch (0.16 cm) of one another.

    A. hairline   B. trapped   C. loose   D. lap

    7.____

8. The purpose of a *slug line* in preparing a mechanical is to indicate

    A. fold lines
    B. the gutter margins
    C. the ruled lines that set type will rest upon
    D. the area that type or artwork is to occupy when set

    8.____

9. The process of spacing letters within a line of type is known as

   A. leading B. kerning C. serifing D. plotting

10. During printing, any rollers — whether inking or dampening — which contact a plate are referred to as

    A. blanket cylinders
    C. form rollers
    B. distributing rollers
    D. impression cylinders

11. Which of the following is LEAST likely to create the need for color correction?

    A. Poor lighting conditions at the time the image was photographed
    B. Incorrect exposure when the image was developed
    C. Wrong type of filter used during photography of the image
    D. Incorrect halftone screen angle

12. Photographic surfaces are made sensitive to light by applying salts of either of the following elements EXCEPT

    A. chromium B. silver C. copper D. iron

13. Which of the following types of proofs are directly from the plate negative films before the plates are exposed?

    A. Prepress proofs
    C. Progressive proofs
    B. Press proofs
    D. Blues

14. Which of the following is/are suitable reproduction applications for intaglio printing?
    I. Photographic images
    II. Large, unbroken solids
    III. Fine lines

    The CORRECT answer is:

    A. I only B. I, II C. II, III D. III only

15. What color drawing ink should be used for the trim lines of Mechanicals?

    A. Cobalt blue
    C. Carmine red
    B. Black
    D. Nonrepro blue

16. In CAD/CAM applications, wireframe modeling

    A. automatically removes lines not normally seen from the angle at which the model is viewed
    B. allows the user to determine a drawn object's center of gravity
    C. divides a drawing into color-coded layers that can be selected individually
    D. represents an object as connected points in space

17. A designer wishes to diminish the shadow in a photograph in order to focus attention on the image. Which of the following techniques should be used?

    A. Halftoning
    C. Toning
    B. Vignetting
    D. Spotting

18. Which of the following shading techniques in image processing is a smooth-shading method that computes different colors at the corners of a polygon and then interpolates these colors across the surfaces? _____ shading.

    A. Phong   B. Gouraud   C. Smooth   D. Flat

19. The obvious DISADVANTAGE associated with acrylic paints concerns their

    A. covering power
    B. water solubility once dry
    C. versatility on different surfaces
    D. ability to receive overlaid washes

20. The ability of an ink to flow during printing operations is expressed in terms of the ink's

    A. depth   B. length   C. wetness   D. viscosity

21. When expressing the dimensions of art during the preparation of a mechanical, which of the following is a standardized practice?

    A. Expressing dimensions in picas rather than inches or centimeters
    B. Keylining dimensions in an overlay
    C. Listing width first, or underlining it
    D. None of the above

22. What is the term used to describe a color-corrected lens that focuses green, blue, and red in the same plane?

    A. Pantone   B. Astigmatic
    C. Polychromatic   D. Apochromatic

23. Drawing table surfaces for use in commercial art applications should have dimensions of at least

    A. 24" x 30"   B. 30" x 40"   C. 36" x 59"   D. 45" x 90"

24. Which of the following are relief printing processes?
    I. Gravure
    II. Letterpress
    III. Flexography
    IV. Intaglio

    The CORRECT answer is:

    A. I, II   B. II, III
    C. III, IV   D. All of the above

25. Which of the following press types is best for handling tints?

    A. Gravure   B. Duplicator offset
    C. Screen   D. Web

KEY (CORRECT ANSWERS)

1. A
2. D
3. D
4. C
5. B

6. A
7. C
8. D
9. B
10. C

11. D
12. C
13. A
14. D
15. A

16. D
17. B
18. B
19. A
20. B

21. C
22. D
23. B
24. B
25. A

ART AND DESIGN

CONTENTS

	Page
I. DESIGN	
1 General	1
2 Form	1
3 Design	1
II. CHARCOAL AND PASTELS	12
4 General	12
5 Tools, Equipment, and Supplies	12
6 Using Charcoal	13
7 Using Pastels	14
8 Safety Precautions	14
9 Therapeutic Aspects	14
III. FINGER PAINTING	14
10 General	14
11 Tools, Supplies, and Equipment	15
12 Processes	17
13 Therapeutic Aspects of Finger Painting	19
IV. OILS	20
14 General	20
15 Tools, Equipment, and Supplies	20
16 Processes	26
17 Safety Precautions	27
18 Therapeutic Aspects of Oil Painting	27
V. STENCILING	28
19 General	28
20 Tools, Equipment, and Supplies	28
21 Process	30
22 Design	32
23 Therapeutic Aspects	33
VI. WATERCOLOR	33
24 General	33
25 Tools, Equipment, and Supplies	33
26 Using Transparent Watercolor	35
27 Opaque Watercolors--Poster Paints	35
28 Therapeutic Aspects	36

ART AND DESIGN

Section I. DESIGN

1. General

Good design and good workmanship are the basic qualities of beautiful and satisfying craftsmanship. As considered here, design includes both the form and the decoration of the piece. The inherent differences in the materials and their response in each of the crafts greatly influence the design of each medium. The slender lines possible with silver, for instance, are not appropriate for ceramics. The realism possible with oil painting cannot be achieved in stencil painting. The craftsman must be familiar with the form and design appropriate to each material and work with the possibilities and within the limitations of the materials he is using. Much of the selection of form and design is, and should be, the choice of the craftsman; much can be done to teach good design to the patients quickly and to guide them to use it. Examples of good design through pictures, samples, and literature will often influence selection, as will appropriate suggestions.

2. Form

Objects have form or shape. All forms are variations and combinations of the four basic shapes: the sphere, the cone, the cube, and the cylinder (fig. 1). Most objects are created to serve a function. For good design, the requirements of the function must be incorporated into the shape. For instance, a pitcher must be designed not only to be pleasing, but it must have a spout which pours well; it must be of an appropriate size for what it is designed to pour; and provision must be made for an easy, secure, and well-balanced grasp of the pitcher. The same principle of design, combined with function, can be applied to weaving. A baby blanket, for instance, must be warm, yet of a lightweight material. The plan or design should also include the use of fine wool rather than of cotton warp or rug wool.

3. Design

When the form (or the plan for it) is complete, additional decoration called applied design can be added to enrich the form. The design does not alter the form, yet it must be planned to suit the form and the material used. Good design should be so clearly related to the basic form that it seems to be a part of it. Design includes line, space, proportion, and color. A well-done design can impart a feeling to the observer. Examples of building blocks of design are given in this manual. Some are familiar to everyone; others may not be so obvious. Consideration of all of them, however, may be of some help, both

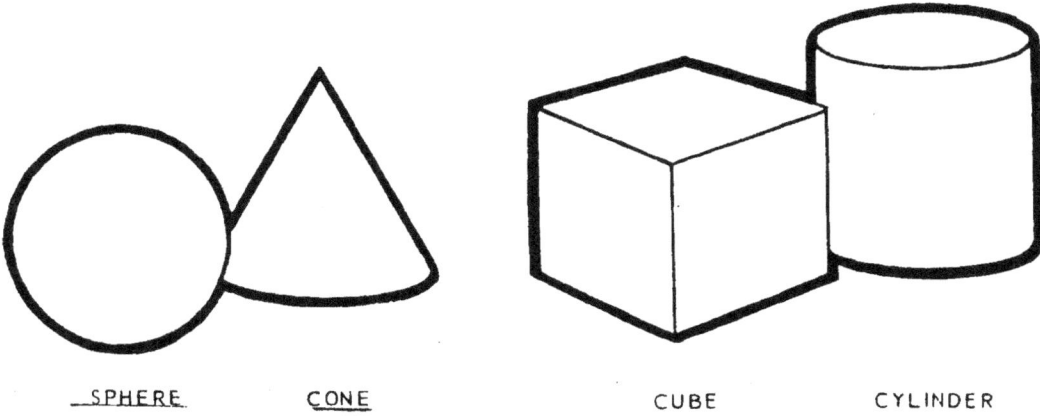

Figure 1. The four basic shapes.

in actually designing and in finding a new appreciation of the work of others.

a. Elements of Design. The following elements of design may be a guide in planning design:

(1) *Line.* The basic lines are straight and curved, but there are many variations. Lines can express moods and qualities.

(*a*) *Straight lines.* These suggest rigidity, precision, hardness, dignity, or strength (fig. 2).

Figure 2. A straight line.

(*b*) *Slightly curved lines.* Femininity, lightness, continuity, gracefulness, and softness are indicated by slightly curved lines (fig. 3).

Figure 3. A slightly curved line.

(*c*) *Curved lines.* Lines which change directions rapidly are active and forceful (fig. 4).

Figure 4. A curved line.

(*d*) *Spiraling curves.* These are dynamic lines which may typify growing things (fig. 5).

Figure 5. A spiraling curve.

(*e*) *Segments of a circle.* Arcs tend to be repetitious and unified, but monotonous (fig. 6).

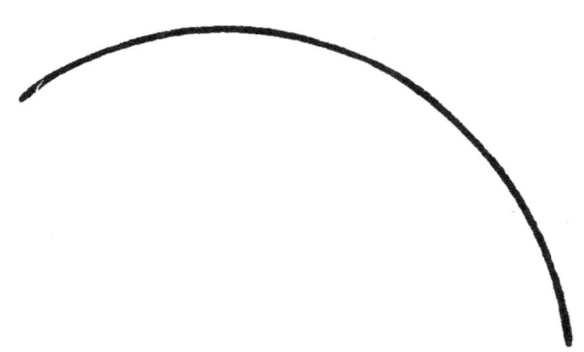

Figure 6. A segment or arc of a circle.

(*f*) *Jagged or zigzag lines.* These lines are disquieting and tend to show nervousness or excitement. They can denote conflict or battle (fig. 7).

Figure 7. A jagged or zigzag line.

(2) *Directions.* In a design, the direction of the line imparts a feeling.

(*a*) *Horizontal.* These lines tend to be restful, quiet, and passive (fig. 8).

(*b*) *Vertical.* Severity, uprightness, strength, dignity, and the feeling of soaring are expressed here (fig. 8).

(*c*) *Oblique.* This line usually needs the support of a line at right angles to it. It expresses movement, action, and excitement (fig. 8).

(3) *Shape.* Shape is a series of lines of different directions defining an area. This area may be round, square, triangular, or another shape (fig. 9).

(4) *Size.* The distance between the lines which define the space may vary, thereby making areas of different sizes. These areas of different sizes result in variety and interest (fig. 10).

(5) *Texture.* All line and shape have texture which may be perceived by sight or touch. Texture is found in nature, but in design it must be planned. The four basic textures are rough-mat, rough-glossy, smooth-mat, and smooth-glossy. These textures may be brought into design by using organic and inorganic materials such as wood, fabric, and glass, or by simulating these textures by stippling, sponging or daubing, spattering, or dry brushing.

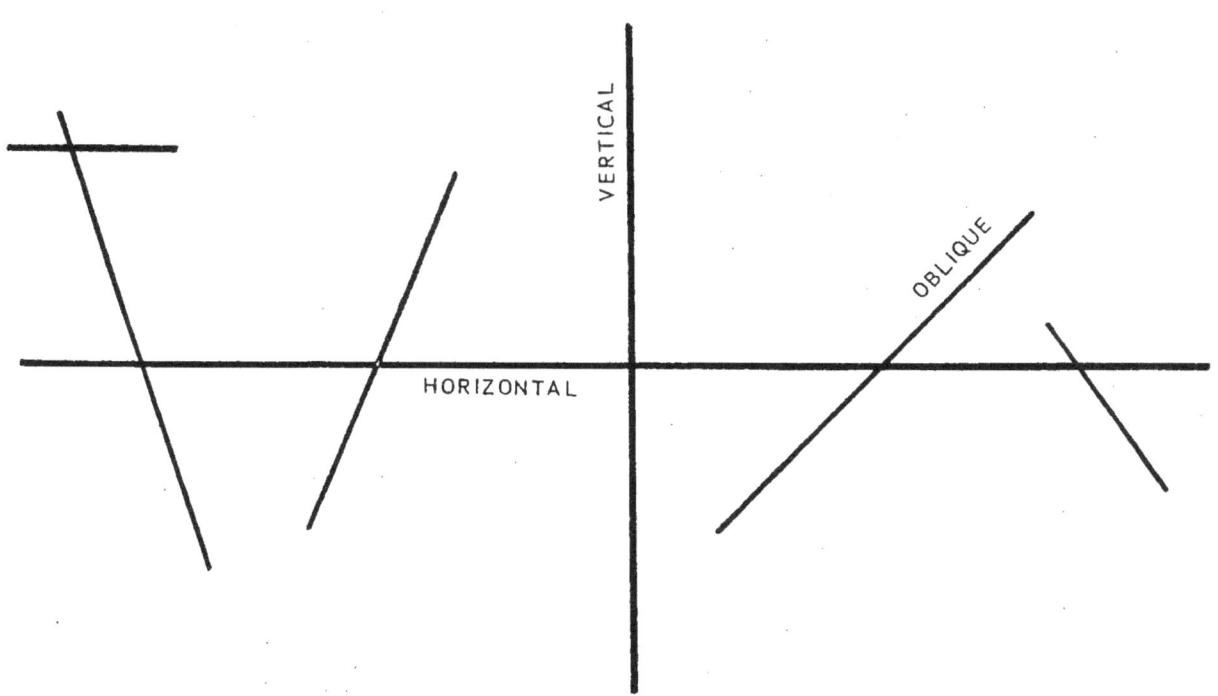

Figure 8. Directions of lines.

Figure 9. Shapes.

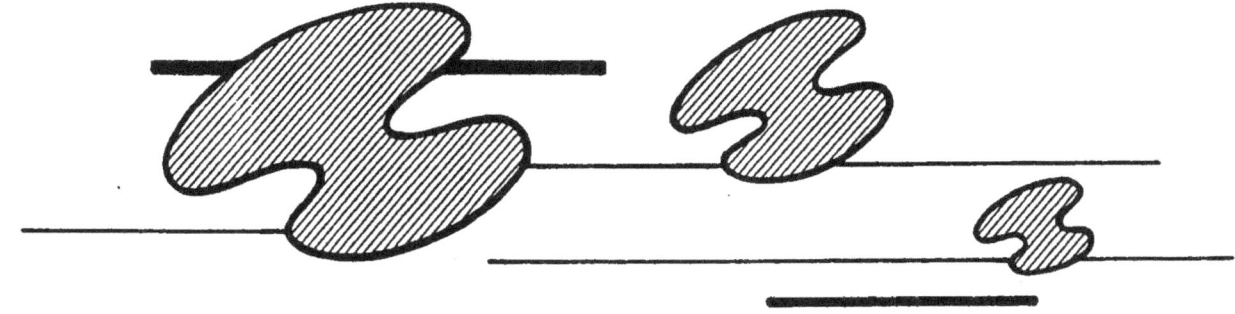

Figure 10. Size.

(6) *Value.* Value refers to the amount of lightness or darkness. The values used in a design impart a feeling to the observer. If the contrast between the darkest and the lightest values is great, the feeling is stimulating and cheerful. If there is little value contrast in the design, the feeling is more dignified or perhaps depressed. In planning a design, then, the mood set by the

value plan must be appropriate to the subject matter. A circus scene should have great contrast, while a scene depicting a meeting of heads of state to decide a serious problem must have less value contrast in order to impart the feeling of the gravity of the occasion.

(7) *Color.* Color is generally recognized as having an effect on mood. This theory has been so accepted that color experts are available for consultation when a factory, an office, or a hospital is to be painted in order to select the coloring that will set the mood desired by management. In planning a design, the color sets the mood, so it must be appropriate to the subject matter. In general, the warm colors (reds, yellows, oranges, and browns) are the ones which

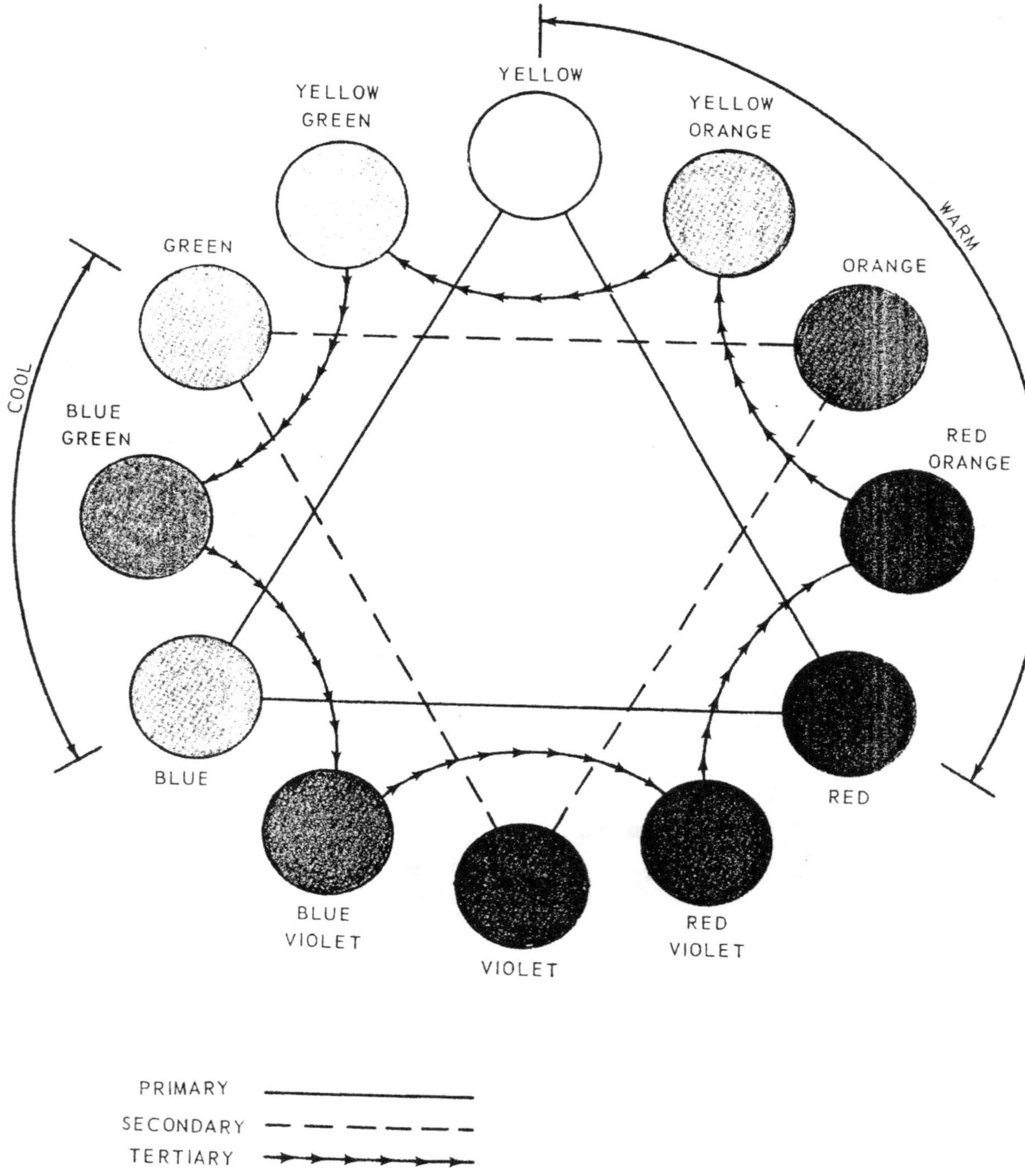

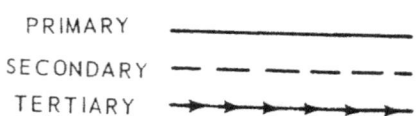

Figure 11. Color wheel.

stand out from their backgrounds and are positive, aggressive, and stimulating (fig. 11); the cool colors (greens, blues, and violets) tend more to recede into the background; they are retiring, aloof, and more negative. White reflects light, whereas black absorbs light. Some specific colors or hues and the feeling they each impart are listed below:

- Red—greatest power of attraction; most popular; exciting, danger, courage, sex.
- Yellow—least popular; bright, sun, gay, lively; darker greenish yellows—sickness, cowardice, treachery.
- Blue—tranquil, serene, hope, sincerity.
- Purple—stately, pompous, rich, royalty.
- Green—restful, faith, freshness, youth.
- White—delicacy, airiness, purity, truth, truce.
- Black—depressing, solemn, death, evil.

This world would be a bizarre place if the three primary colors were all that were available (fig. 11). Mixing color is a fascinating skill, but only the very basic principles can be considered here. One theory of mixing colors is diagramed in the color wheel, which is made by bending the spectrum into a closed circle (fig. 11).

(a) *Primary colors.* These are the three colors from which all other colors are derived. Unmixed, they have the highest strength and intensity possible—this is referred to as chroma. The three primary colors are—

- red
- yellow
- blue

(b) *Secondary colors.* Mixing two primary colors gives the secondary colors—

- red and yellow—orange
- yellow and blue—green
- blue and red—violet

(c) *Tertiary or intermediate colors.* These are a mixture of one primary and one secondary color—

- red and violet—red violet
- red and orange—red orange
- blue and violet—blue violet
- blue and green—blue green
- yellow and orange—yellow orange
- yellow and green—yellow green

(d) *Neutrals.* Neutrals are black and white and the many grays produced by mixing black and white in different amounts. Neutrals with just a little color added are near neutrals. Mixing a color with a neutral, either black or white, lowers the intensity of the color.

(e) *Grayed color.* When a color is mixed with a color from the opposite side of the color wheel (called its complement), the result is a grayed color. Red and green, for instance, result in a grayed or near-neutral color.

(f) *Tints.* Colors mixed with whites produce a tint. Red mixed with white produces pink.

(g) *Shades.* Colors mixed with black produce shades. Red-orange mixed with black produces brown.

(h) *Broken color mixing.* This is the old and recently revised technique of placing small units of different colors next to each other without mixing them. The result is more alive and intense than is obtained by actually mixing the colors together.

(i) *Color schemes or combinations.* Colors are combined in many ways. Some combinations are almost traditional because of their constant, age-old, and frequent use. Other combinations, less familiar and less comfortable, are dictated by fashion and fad, so they come and go. The designer must be free to use any combinations he wishes in order to impart the message or feeling that he has in mind. Color schemes that may be used in a design or that may serve to suggest other possibilities are shown below:

- *Monochrome.* Only a combination of one color or hue in different tints, tones, and shades is used.
- *Analogous.* One primary color is used with its neighboring secondary and tertiary colors (*for example,* blue with blue-green and green).
- *Complementary.* Only the two colors opposite each other on the color wheel are used in the design (*for example,* red and green).
- *Split complementary.* One color and either one or both of the colors to the right and left of its complement are used (*for example,* red with yellow-green and/or blue-green).
- *Triad.* Three colors which are equidistant apart on the color wheel are used in a design (*for example,* green, violet, and orange).

b. *Principles of Design.* The principles of design are the fundamental laws of relationship or the plans of organization which determine the way the elements of design are combined for certain effects.

(1) *Repetition.* In repetition, the difference

between the units is in their position or placement.

(a) *Exact repetition.* One unit is repeated without even a difference of space between units (fig. 12). It is monotonous and uninteresting because of absence of variety.

Figure 12. Exact repetition.

(b) *Varied repetition.* One unit is repeated, but its direction, size, texture, value, and color may be varied (fig. 13).

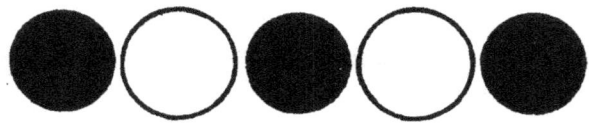

Figure 13. Varied repetition.

(c) *Alternate repetition.* One unit followed by a second (or more) unit that is different, giving rhythm and variety (fig. 14).

Figure 14. Alternate repetition.

(d) *Number of repetitions.* An odd number of repetitions is more interesting than an even number (fig. 15).

(2) *Harmony.* Harmony is the proper relationship of the parts to the whole.

(a) *Harmony of elements.* The units are similar in one or more of the design elements (fig. 16).

(b) *Harmony of function.* Harmony of dissimilar objects is occasioned by their common association together (fig. 17).

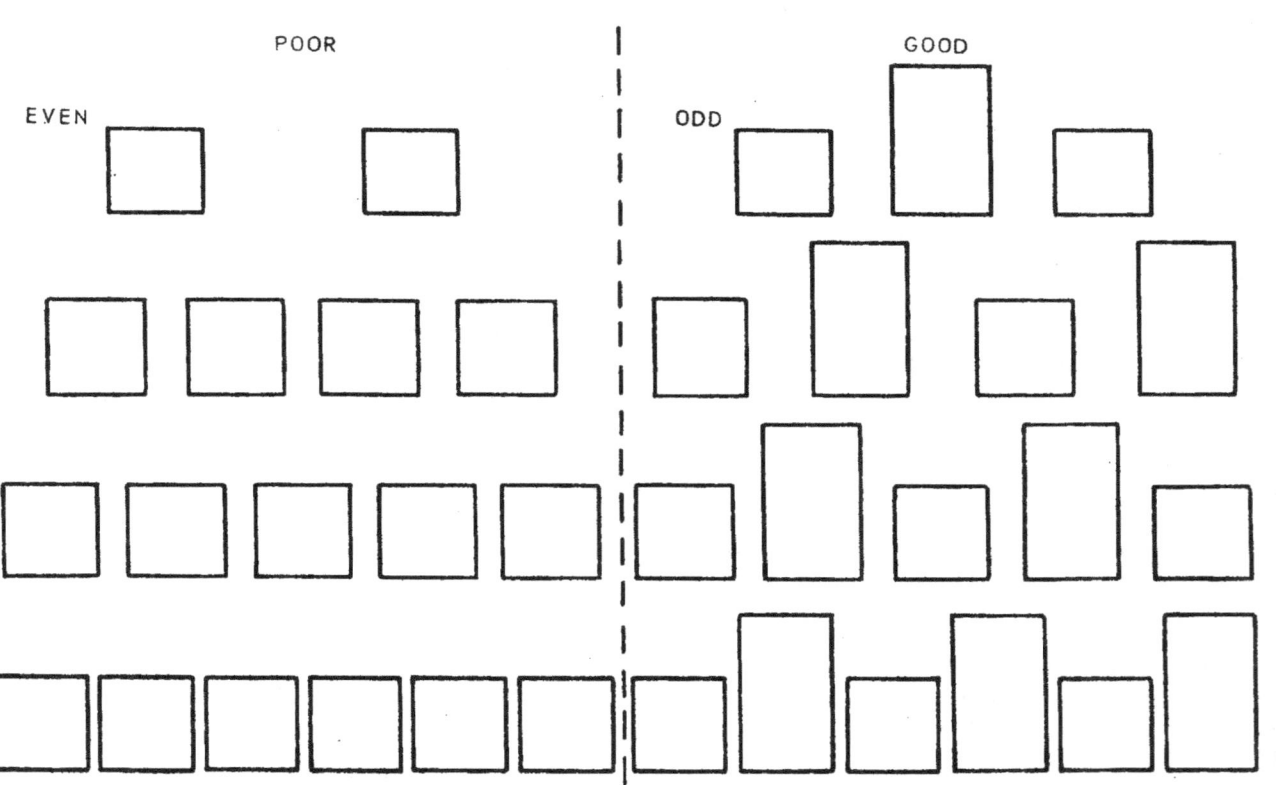

Figure 15. Number of repetitions.

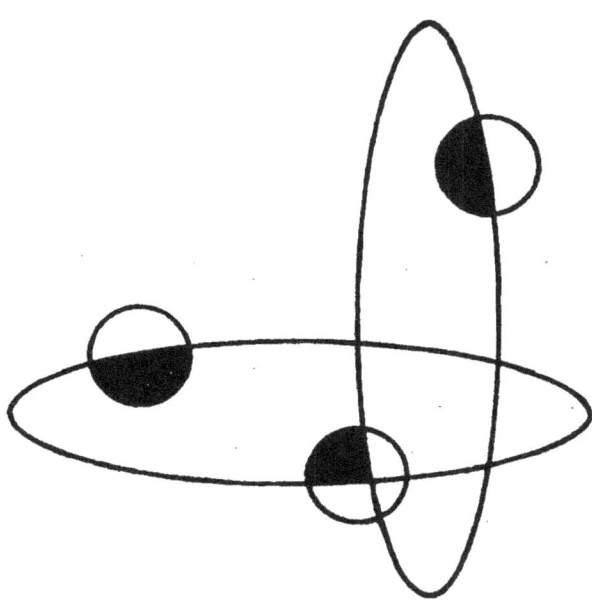

Figure 16. Harmony of elements.

Figure 18. Harmony of symbolism.

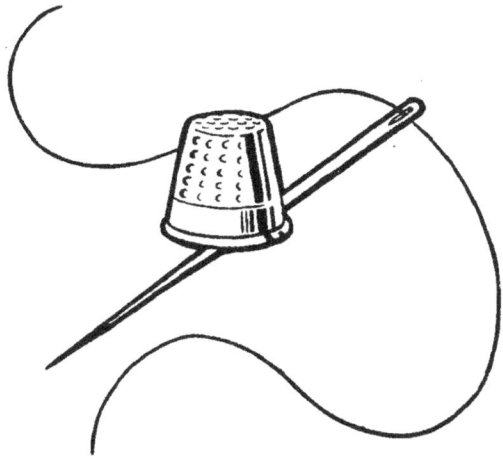

Figure 17. Harmony of function.

Figure 19. Gradation of sequence.

(c) *Harmony of symbolism.* Harmony occurs also in the symbolism of subject matter; *for example*, a rabbit in a hat conveys the idea of a magician (fig. 18).

(3) *Gradation.* This is a type of harmony in which the relationship is one of space and movement rather than of ideas.

(a) *Steps in sequence.* Elements are connected by a series of harmonious steps (fig. 19).

(b) *Radiation.* Gradation of directions may be shown by radiation of lines (fig. 20).

(4) *Contrast.* Such things as opposing lines, directions, shapes, and colors make contrast in design.

(a) *Discord.* This is complete contrast with no similar design elements. The units are totally unrelated and the result is garish and poor design (fig. 21).

(b) *Variety or mild contrast.* Some units

have harmonious design elements and others have contrast. This is essential to good design as it stimulates interest and arouses excitement (fig. 22).

Figure 20. *Gradation of direction.*

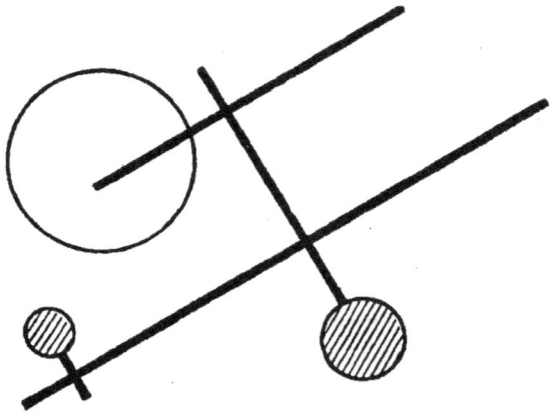

Figure 22. *Contrast—variety.*

(5) *Unity.* This is a oneness and a cohesion of design brought about by the other design principles (repetition, harmony, gradation, variety, dominance, and balance).

(6) *Dominance.* One unit of a design must dominate the other units (fig. 23).

(7) *Balance.* The feeling that the designer wishes to give determines the type of balance used.

(a) *Formal or symmetrical balance.* A balance on opposite sides of an axis of one or

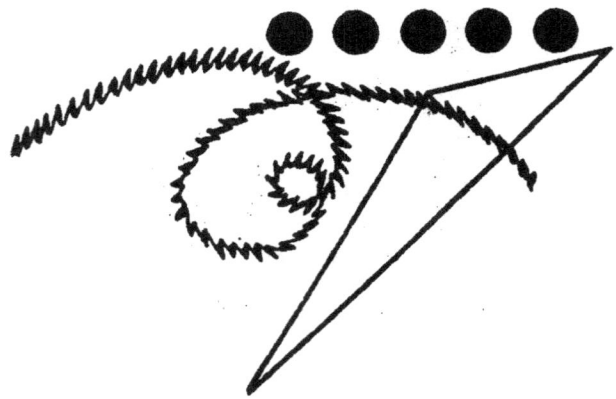

Figure 21. *Contrast—discord.*

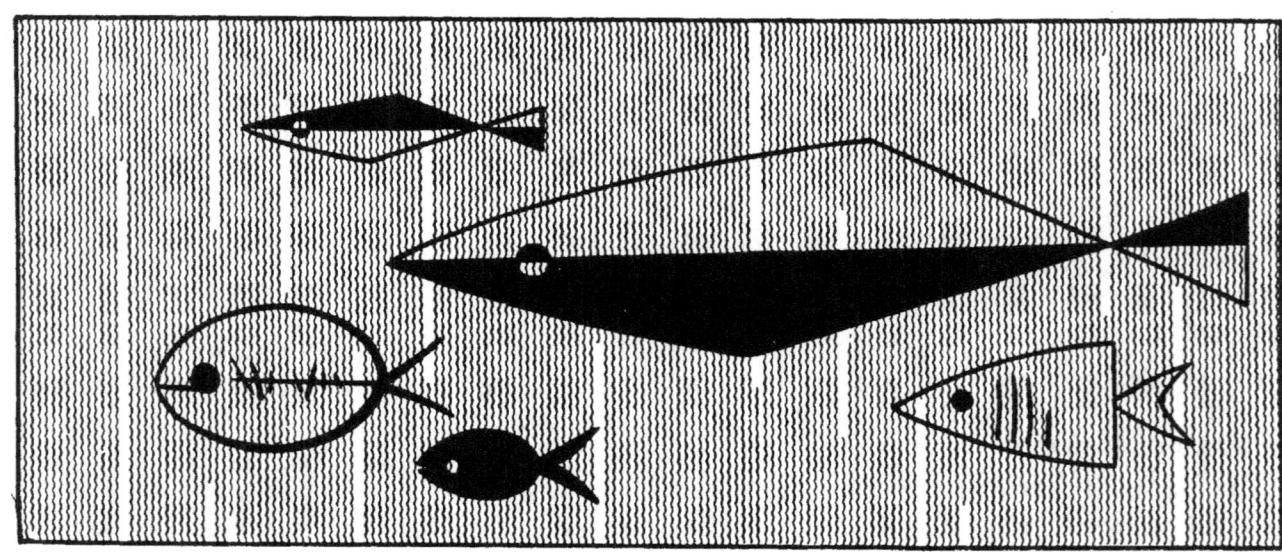

Figure 23. *Dominance.*

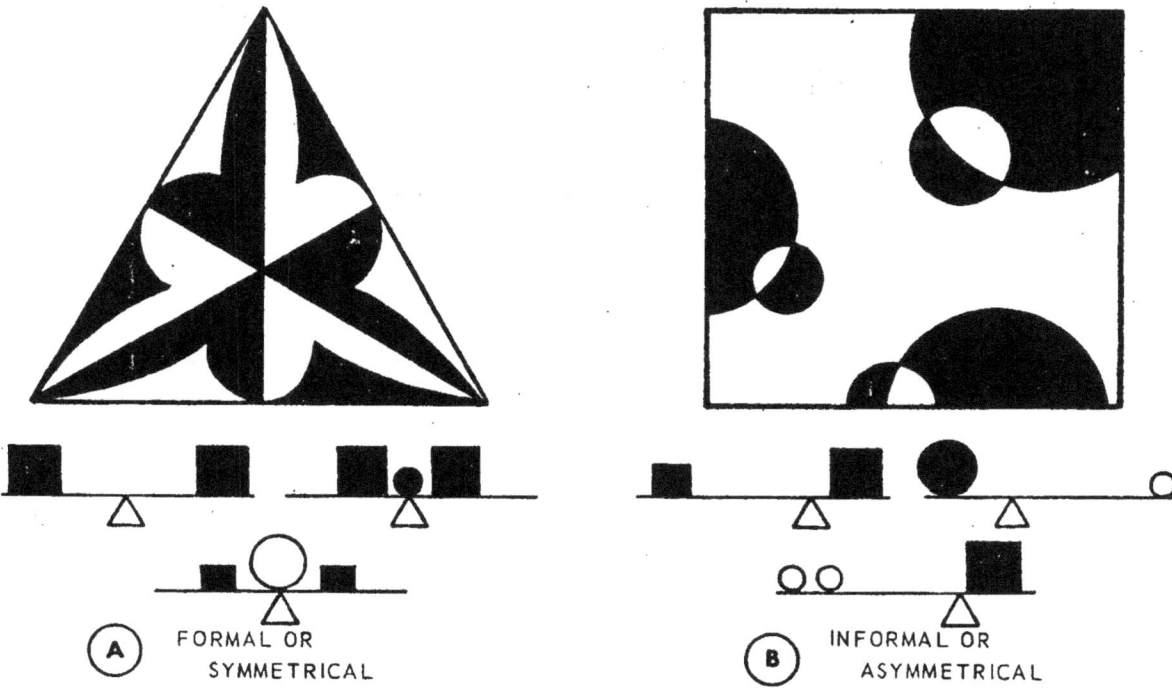

Figure 24. Balance.

more units by identical or very similar units. This is classical balance, which is stately, dignified, and serene (A, fig. 24).

(b) *Informal or assymmetrical balance.* A balance on opposite sides of an axis of one or more units by dissimilar or contrasting units. This more modern type of balance is informal and less peaceful in feeling, but more interesting (B, fig. 24).

(8) *Proportion.* This is a comparison of intervals of length and area which brings about a harmonic relation between parts or different things of the same kind.

(a) *Breaking of a surface.* A good breaking of surface has unit and variety produced by parts which contrast in size and in shape, yet are related to each other and to the original surface. Although a division at the center is perfect unity, it is monotonous and uninteresting, so halfway points should be avoided (fig. 25).

(b) *Horizontal division of an area.* Unequal division of an area can serve to give emphasis in a picture (fig. 26).

(c) *Ratios between height and width.* Obvious ratios between height and width, such as 1 to 1 and 2 to 1 are undesirable. Good ratios are 2 to 5, 3 to 8, 7 to 10, etc.

c. *Methods of Design Development.* The basic lines in a(1) above can be developed into motifs or designs in many ways, some of which are suggested to provide a background for further development. *For example*, several different meth-

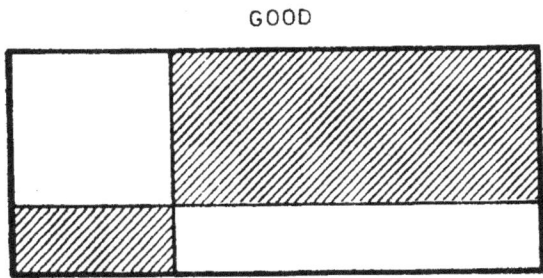
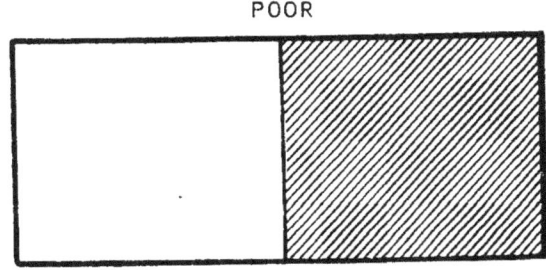

Figure 25. Division of surface.

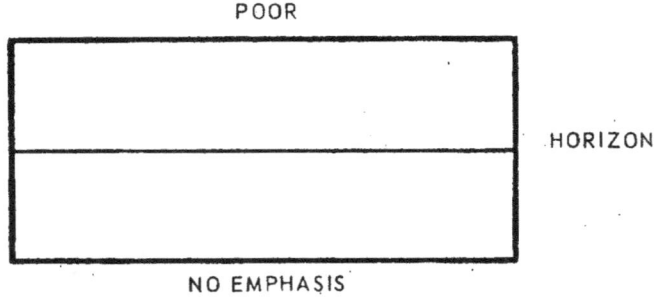
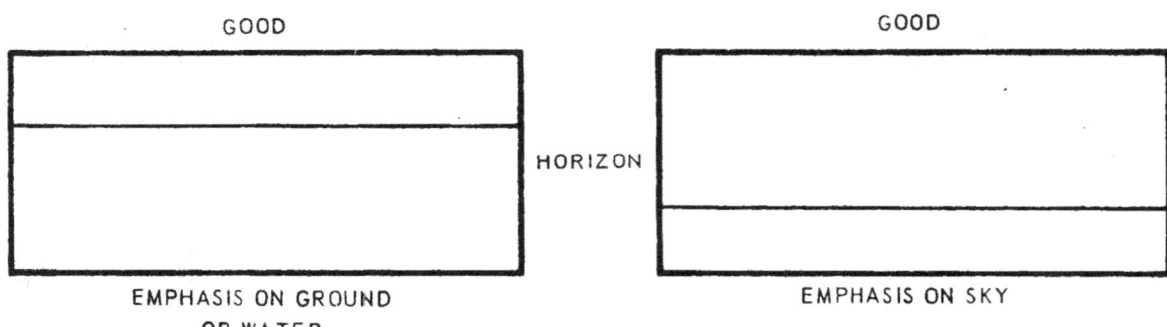

Figure 26. Horizontal division of an area.

ods of treating the slightly curved line are shown below. Other lines and simple motifs might respond in as interesting a way to at least some of the methods of treatment.

(1) *Repeat.* The slightly curved line was repeated to form a very simple border design (fig. 27). It can also be repeated to make an allover pattern. Here the line has been combined ((2) below) with an arc and repeated laterally and horizontally to form a well-related, allover pattern (fig. 28).

(2) *Combine.* Two or more simple elements can be combined to develop an effective design (fig. 29).

(3) *Expand.* The curved line is effective in a design if it is expanded (fig. 30).

(4) *Condense.* The same element is entirely different when it is condensed (fig. 31).

(5) *Change direction.* Changing the direction of the line can be developed into an entirely different border design (fig. 32). This could also be made into an allover pattern.

Figure 27. A simple border design.

Figure 28. Allover pattern.

Figure 29. Combining elements.

Figure 30. Expanded curved line.

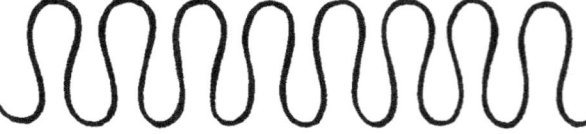

Figure 31. Condensed curved line.

Figure 32. Changing direction.

d. *Interpretation of Design.* It is the privilege of the designer to interpret the design as he wishes in order to impart the feeling that he wants people to get from his design. Some of the most common treatments of the same theme are given below:

(1) *Naturalistic.* Record what is seen exactly as it appears in nature without artistic stylization (fig. 33).

NATURALISTIC

CONVENTIONAL

ABSTRACT

GEOMETRIC

Figure 33. Interpretation.

(2) *Conventional.* In this interpretation, the artist reduces the details, thereby simplifying the naturalistic interpretation (fig. 33).

(3) *Abstract.* Here, the motif is reduced to simple shapes and forms, which represent rather than record (fig. 33).

(4) *Geometric.* This interpretation is completely angular—without the use of curved lines (fig. 33).

Section II. CHARCOAL AND PASTELS

4. General

In both charcoal and pastel work, pigment in the form of chalklike materials, is applied to textured paper. The texture of the paper plays an important role in the texture and feeling of the work.

CAUTION

Because of the nature of this medium, the work produces a considerable amount of dust. It is therefore suggested that papers be spread under the working area, that the artist be protected by an all-over apron, and that provisions be made for frequent wiping of the fingers, especially if shading is to be done with the fingers.

5. Tools, Equipment, and Supplies

a. Chamois Skin. The chamois skin is used for blending large areas in both pastel and charcoal work.

b. Charcoal. Several types of charcoal are available; inherent in each is a certain softness or hardness or a size which provides textures desired by the artist. A type that is often used is vine charcoal (fig. 34). Vine charcoal is not pressed but is in the natural shape of the vine. It is usually softer than pressed and is very fragile to handle. It is available in both large and small sizes.

c. Drawing Board. A drawing board with a smooth surface is important to have when using either pastels or charcoal.

d. Fixative or Fixatif. Because charcoal and pastels are powdery, they must be sprayed with a clear, quick-drying, varnish-based liquid to protect them from rubbing off the paper. Two types of fixatives are used—

(1) Workable fixative dries quickly to a mat finish and may be worked over with charcoal or pastels. It is used to set the work before it is finished.

(2) Spraying with regular fixative is done after the work is completed, to protect the surface from rubbing and from smudges. It cannot be worked over; it is waterproof and crystal clear; and it is available in either gloss or mat finish.

e. Fixative Sprayer. Both charcoal and pastels

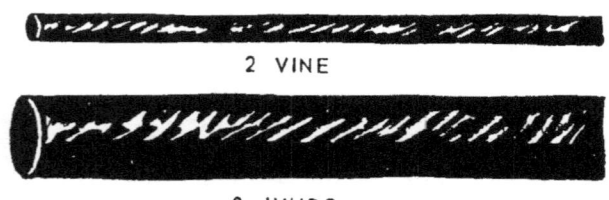

Figure 34. Vine charcoal.

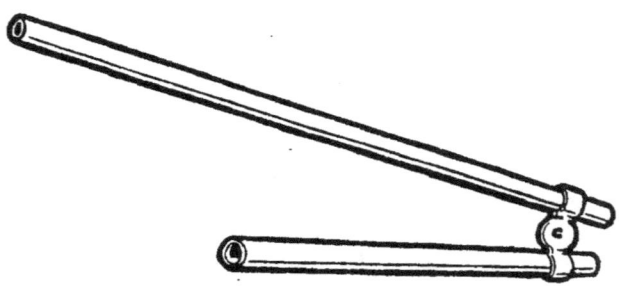

FOLDING ATOMIZER

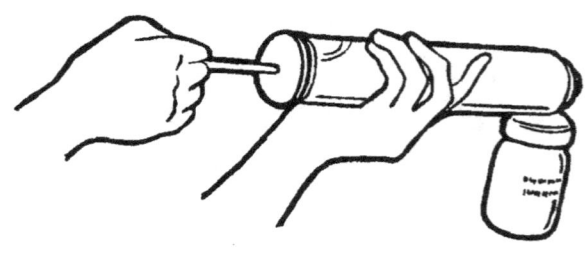

HAND PUMP

Figure 35. Sprayers.

are sprayed with a material to keep them from smearing. The atomizer (fig. 35) is put into the bottom of fixative; blowing into it makes a spray. A different type of sprayer is also shown in figure 35. Pressurized cans of fixative are also available.

f. Kneaded Rubber. This soft rubber can be kneaded in the fingers to keep a clean working surface ready to cut out highlights on a drawing.

g. Paper. Several types of paper are used in this work, and some are available in pads as well as in sheets. The choice depends upon the needs of the patients and upon the texture. Newsprint can be used quite successfully for practice work. Following is a list of papers which can be used:

(1) Tinted charcoal.

(2) Suede paper.

(3) Sanded paper in 7–0, 8–0, or 9–0.

h. Pastels. Pastels are usually packaged in sets or single colors in a box of 6 or 12 (fig. 36). They are available in different degrees of hardness and in many colors, each with varying percentages of white mixed in the pastel. For use with patients in occupational therapy, it is usually economical to purchase sets of 12 to 30 colors. Then, when necessary, boxes of the most used colors are purchased.

i. Sandpaper Block. A pad of medium sandpaper mounted on wood is used for keeping a point on charcoal, pencils, and pastels (fig. 37).

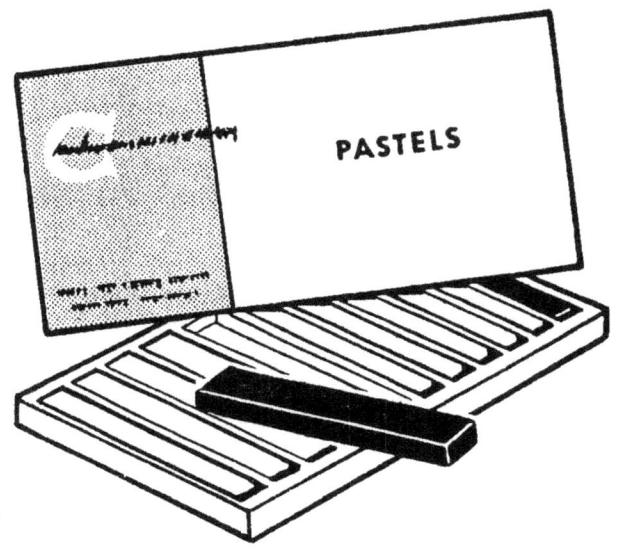

Figure 36. Small set of pastels.

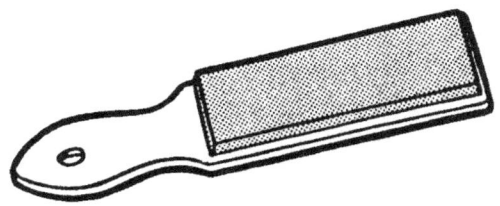

Figure 37. Sandpaper block.

j. Stumps. Stumps are soft gray paper rolled to form a point to use when blending or shading charcoal or pastels in small areas. They may be double-pointed or single-pointed (fig. 38). Stumps may also be made of felt or of leather.

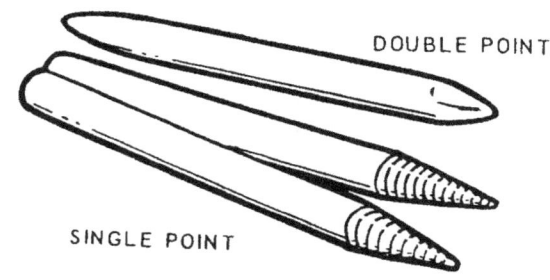

Figure 38. Stumps.

6. Using Charcoal

Charcoal is used to plan areas and to sketch in objects in preparation for other drawings. It is also an interesting medium to use in itself. In charcoal work, the subject is viewed as being composed of planes, with light and shadows within the planes. The following steps may be used as a guide in doing charcoal work:

a. With mostly straight lines, divide the area to be used, then sketch in the subject. Use the chamois to erase unwanted lines.

b. Darken the shadowed areas. Do this in two ways—

(1) Draw them in, using a sharpened charcoal stick with medium pressure, stroking in one direction.

(2) Rough the dark areas in with charcoal, then shade with the finger for the large areas and with a stump for the small areas.

c. Use the stumps for softening hard edges or for creating half tones.

d. Use the kneaded eraser to clear the paper of charcoal and thereby pick out the highlights.

7. Using Pastels

Pastels are handled in about the same way as charcoal but with the added challenge of color. There are seemingly innumerable colors and variations from which to choose. It is also possible to superimpose one color over another to get subtle shadings. Each artist has his own method of working, but the following steps may be used as a guide:

a. Plan the space by drawing guidelines roughly to get proportions and general form. This drawing is done with charcoal or with a neutral color pastel. Throughout the work, the guidelines must be retained as long as there is a need for them.

b. Start filling in the cloors, using the brighter ones first, as they can be neutralized later. A good policy is to use cool tones for shadows and warm tones in the lighter areas. A color may be altered by working over it with another.

c. Along with the coloring, work with the center of interest to bring it out. An outline of charcoal or browns may be used to emphasize an area. Conform the direction of the stroke to the lines of the object.

d. Blend color with the fingers or a chamois skin in the large areas and with a stump in the smaller areas.

e. Set the color several times with workable fixative. This is done best by spraying at a distance of 20 to 24 inches and using several light coats rather than one heavy one.

f. Step back frequently to appraise the work.

g. Bring out details, outlines, and sharp edges with charcoal or with a finely pointed pastel.

h. When the work is completed, tap the paper to remove loose particles of pastel, then protect the picture with fixatif or frame it, using glass as a covering but with it built up about 1/4 inch from the drawing.

8. Safety Precautions

There is no danger inherent in the tools or the material except possible irritation from the dust. However, other material should probably be used when patients have a pulmonary problem.

9. Therapeutic Aspects

Both charcoal and pastels are used mainly with psychiatric and general medical and surgical patients. Charcoal is enough like a pencil and pastels are enough like crayons that an apprehensive patient may feel more at home with them than with oils or watercolors. Enhancing the basic familiarity of these modalities is the fact that they are sufficiently different to work with to present a challenge and thereby hold the interest of the patient.

a. Psychiatric Patients. Both charcoal and pastels provide an excellent means of expression for the patient. They are easy to work with; they respond in texture to the feelings of the patient; there is a good selection of color (pastels); and working with them is fast, rather thn labored. The material is sufficiently inexpensive that, when an error is made or when one quick drawing is completed, the page can be torn off and a new one started. The patients often respond to the freedom of not being committed to a labored setup of oils or watercolors or to staying on one canvas and therefore feel free to express ideas and moods.

b. Physical Disability Patients. Neither charcoal nor pastels are used to any extent in the treatment of patients with physical disabilities.

c. General Medical and Surgical Patients. The freedom and familiarity of these modalities often lure patients who have had no art training to try their skills with either pastels or charcoal. They can either stay with them or perhaps, with the confidence they gain, go on to other materials. Because of the dust inherent in this work, it is not recommended for use by bed patients.

Section III. FINGER PAINTING

10. General

Finger painting is perhaps the most fluid, yet the least demanding, means of expression in the art field. Learning to use tools is not a problem; errors are easily erased and an entirely new beginning is provided with a wipe of the hand. The paintings can be framed and used as pictures, or made into book jackets, used to cover wastebaskets, or made into greeting cards or note paper; the larger sheets can even provide interesting paper for wrapping gifts.

11. Tools, Supplies, and Equipment

a. Iron. An ordinary iron is used to straighten the paper after the painting is dry.

b. Newspapers. Spread newspapers provide an ideal place for drying the paintings.

c. Paint. Finger paint is a smooth, paste-like water-soluble, nonpoisonous material which comes in a variety of colors (about eight). Sets include finger paint paper, wooden sticks for taking paint from the jars; and small jars of paint in red, yellow, green, blue, brown, and black. It can be purchased in different quantities; the most economical depends upon the quantity of paint used. It is available in half pint, pint, quart, and gallon sizes. Sometimes it is more economical and more practical to make finger paint. Following are several recipes, including both cooked and uncooked:

(1) *Cooked finger paint.*
   (a) 1/2 box laundry starch
       1 quart boiling water
       1/2 cup talcum powder
       1 1/2 cup soapflakes
       Oil of wintergreen
       Tempera or poster paint

Dissolve the laundry starch in cold water, then add a quart of boiling water to the mixture while stirring it vigorously. Cook the starch and water mixture until it has a glossy appearance. Set it aside to cool. While it is cooling, add 1/2 cup talcum powder and, after the mixture becomes tepid, stir in 1 1/2 cups soapflakes. Add a few drops of oil of wintergreen as a preservative. Pour the finger paint into jars, then add thinned tempera or poster paint for the colors desired.

   (b) 1/2 cup laundry starch
       Cold water
       2 cups boiling water
       Food coloring or tempera paint

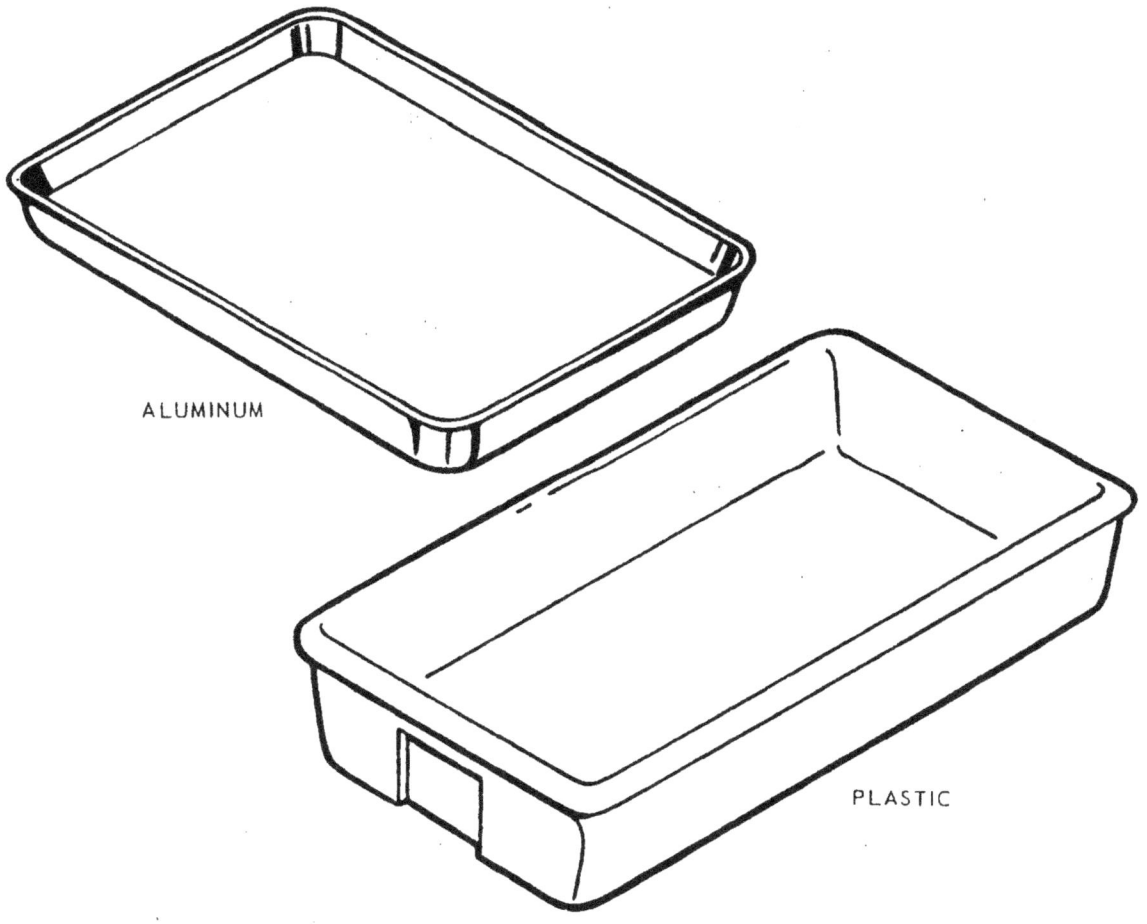

Figure 39. Finger paint trays.

Mix the starch with enough cold water to make a thick, smooth paste. Add the boiling water; stirring constantly. Cook until thick and clear—keep stirring. Cool. Add colors. Two tablespoons sodium benzoate will help preserve the paint.

(2) *Uncooked finger paint.*
 (a) 3 cups cold water
  1 cup wheat paste (wallpaper paste)
  1 teaspoon dry or liquid tempera

Stir the wheat paste into the cold water, little by little. Add the tempera paint.

 (b) Liquid starch
  Dry tempera powder or crumbled chalk
  A little cold water

Use the liquid starch as it comes from the jar. Add a little cold water to aid the spreadability of the starch. Mix in powdered tempera to the color consistency desired.

d. Pans for Water. If there is no sink in the working area, pans of water (fig. 39) large enough to pull the 16-inch by 22-inch paper through will be needed. Other pans to hold water for washing the hands will also be used.

e. Paper. Finger-paint paper is strong when wet and has a glossy surface. It is cut in sheets, usually 16 inches by 22 inches, and is available by the sheet, in a package of 100 sheets, or by the ream. White shelf paper is a good substitute for commercial finger paint paper.

f. Rags. These are essential for wiping up paint.

g. Sponge. A sponge is used to clean one color from an area of the paper before another color is added.

h. Spoons. The paint is taken from the jar to the paper with a spoon. Tongue depressors are a good substitute and they do not need to be cleaned.

i. Table. Finger painting should be done on a table with a smooth top which will not be damaged by water. If one is not available, masonite cut larger than the paper is a good substitute.

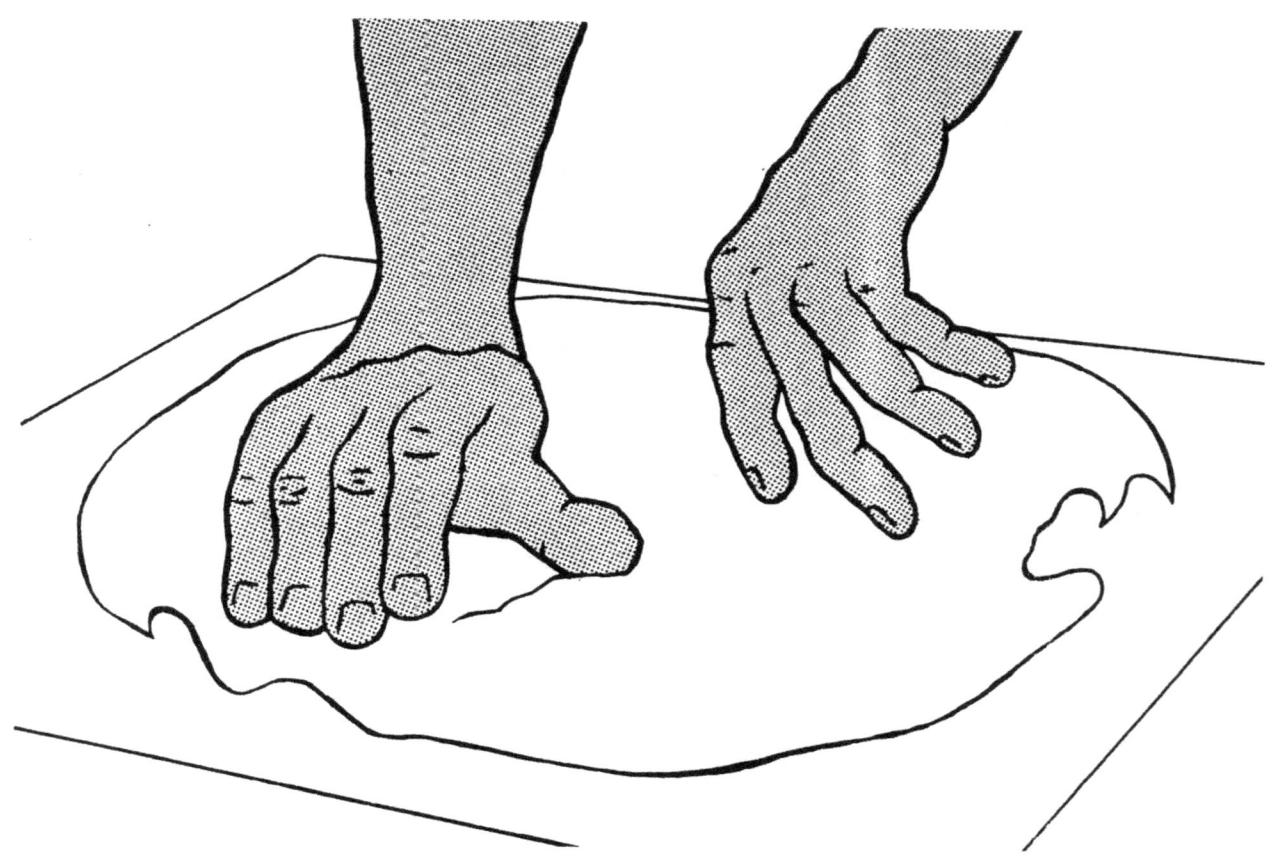

Figure 40. Spreading the finger paint.

12. Processes

Before any painting is done, the area must be protected from both paint and water. To foster freedom of motion and relaxation, the artist's clothes should also be well protected.

a. Wet the Paper. Run the paper through the water to wet it on both sides. Do not soak the paper as it will lose strength. Lay the wet paper, with the glazed side up, on the working surface. Smooth all air bubbles from under the paper by picking up one end and stroking the paper in the direction of the raised end.

b. Put Paint on the Paper. Put about a heaping teaspoonful of the desired color paint in the center of the wet paper. With the hand, spread the paint over the entire sheet of paper (fig. 40), smoothing out any lumps of paint at the same time. In order to cover the edges of the paper with paint, the smoothing might extend over the paper and onto the table at the edge. If the paint begins to get dry, sprinkle on a little clear water and smooth the paint again.

c. Experiment With the Paint. Begin to try the effect of various parts of the hand and arms in the paint. There is no routine or pattern to follow; this is a fluid modality and the artist works as he wishes. Some suggestions to enlarge the scope of effects which can be obtained with this type of painting are listed and illustrated below.

(1) The heel of the hand is used here for pushing the paint around and getting the rhythmic effect. Flower forms can be made by twisting with the heel of the hand (fig. 41).

(2) Large leaves can be formed by using an upward stroke with the side of the hand (fig. 42).

(3) The little finger and the fingernails give fine detail (fig. 43).

(4) The entire forearm may be used for bold, sweeping effects (fig. 44).

(5) The clenched fist drawn, twisted, or set on the paint provides additional interesting stro (fig. 45).

d. Do a Painting. After thorough exploration has acquainted the artist with the freedom and the possibilities of the modality, he is ready to give attention to composition. The artist should not be bound by realism or meaning necessarily, as just "feeling" can be expressed well with finger painting. When one composition is completed,

Figure 41. Using the heel of the hand.

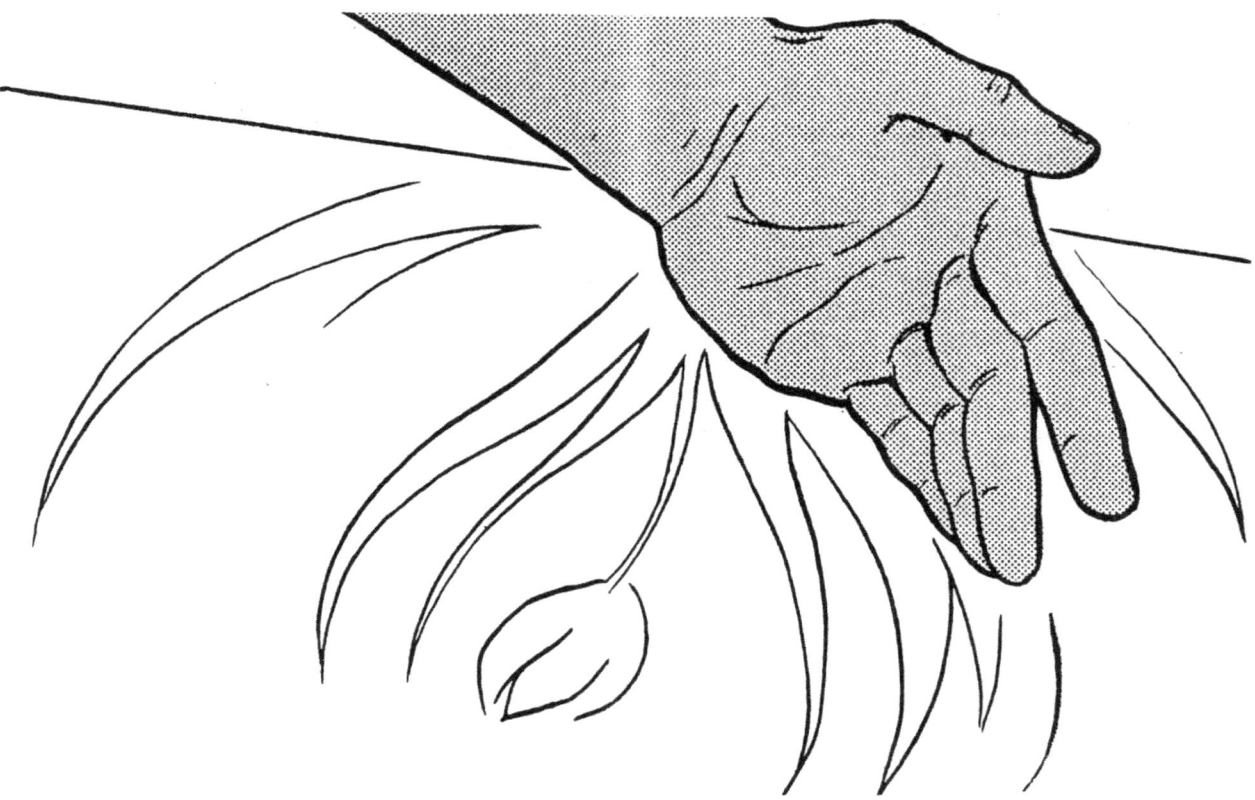

Figure 42. Using the side of the hand.

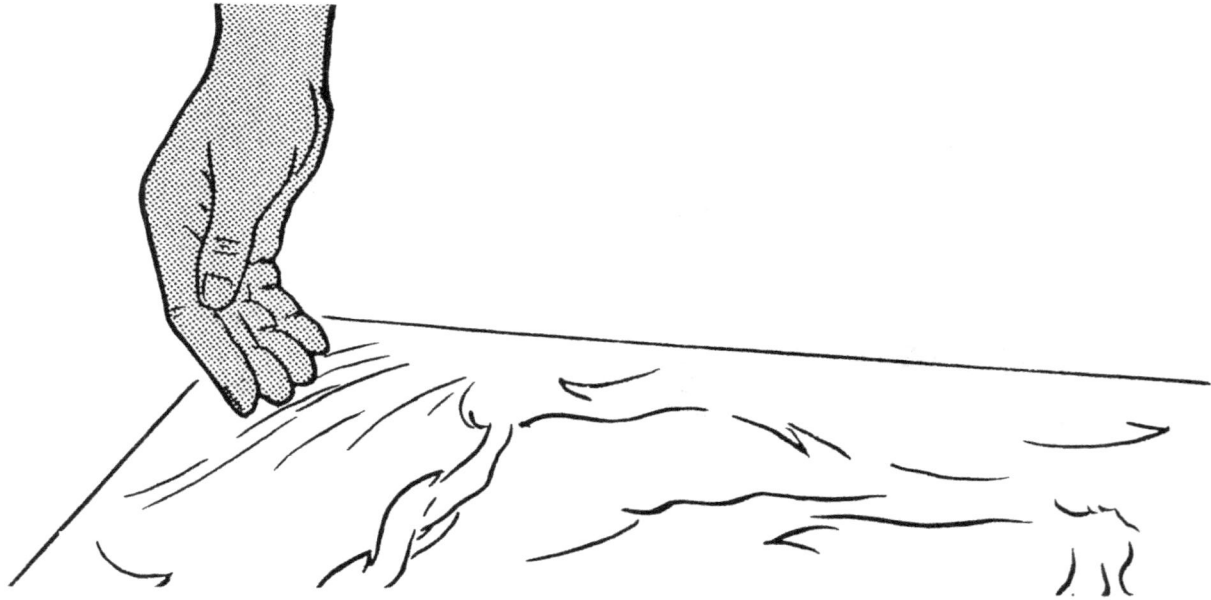

Figure 43. Using finger motions for details.

another can be done in the same way, but perhaps with another color of paint.

e. Add Colors. In finger painting, color is secondary to form and shape. It is possible to use several colors in one painting. Blending of colors is done with the hand. To add a new color and keep it clear, put a little of the new color on the table, moisten it, and rub it free from lumps,

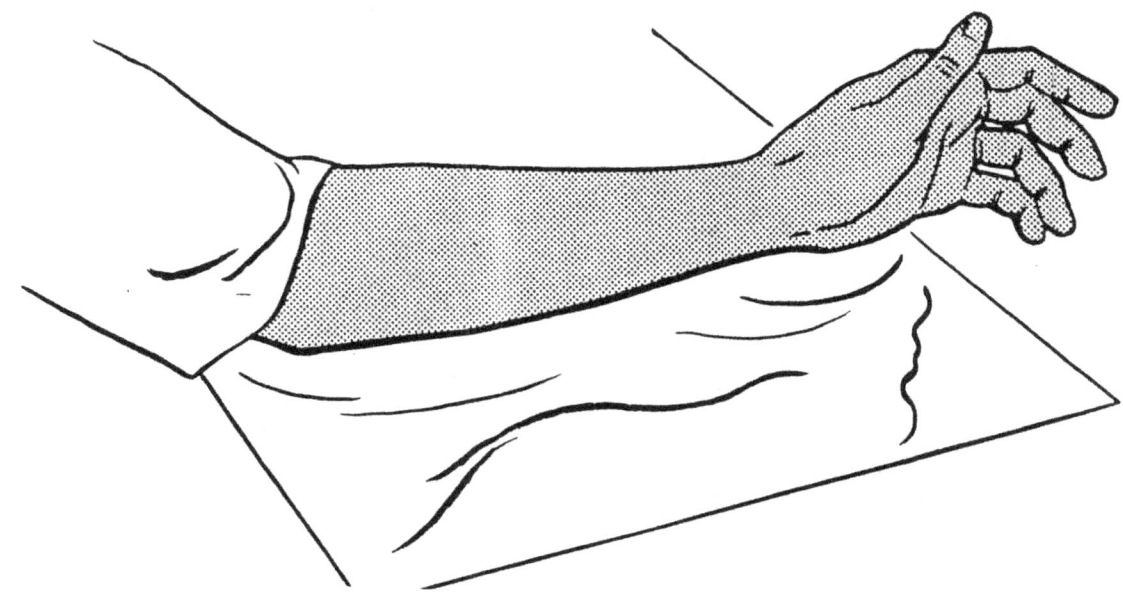

Figure 44. Using the entire forearm.

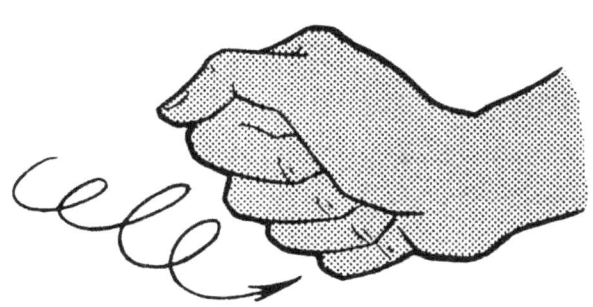

Figure 45. Using the fist.

ready for use. Clean the desired spot in the composition by wiping it free of the first color with a rag or sponge, then put the prepared new color in the spot. Proceed then to give the paint the desired form, taking care to keep the background color from mixing with the new color.

f. Finish the Painting. Lift the painting carefully by two corners and peel it from the table or board. Put it on newspaper to dry. After it is thoroughly dry, press it on the reverse side with a hot iron. A complete finger painting is shown in figure 46.

13. Therapeutic Aspects of Finger Painting

a. Physically Disabled Patients. Finger painting is sometimes used to encourage or to demonstrate beginning upper extremity motion. The motion may be the same in each extremity; it may be reciprocal; or the motions may not be related in any way. The result of any motion can be pleasing and therefore gratifying.

b. Psychiatric Patients. Finger painting is valuable in this field because of its complete freedom. The patient is able to express what he feels without the inhibiting influence of tools or preconceived ideas, usually of what is appropriate for that modality. Because of this, more of "the patient" is apt to be put on paper. Verbalization during the painting is important; anything said should be reported when the picture is shown to the psychiatrist.

c. General Medical and Surgical Patients. This may be an interesting and unusual modality for long-term patients. They may enjoy the development of different ways to use the paintings.

Figure 46. Completed finger painting.

Section IV. OILS

14. General

Oil has been the basic medium in the art field for over 500 years and there is good reason for this popularity. Oils achieve an unparalleled depth of tone and intensity of color at the start, during the painting, and after completion. Oils dry slowly, so there is time to work and to correct errors before the paint becomes dry. Rewards are obtained from other than the completed painting. Just getting out in the open with a project and a goal is a relaxing change for the person who must work within the confines of a building most of the time. Painting provides a relief from the spectator role and enables the painter to match his ever-developing skills against the complexities of what he sees. Perhaps the greatest intrigue of all is that art is always a pursuit, impossible to catch up with no matter how skilled one becomes.

15. Tools, Equipment, and Supplies

a. Brushes. Most artists stress the importance of buying the best brushes that one can afford. When purchasing for one's own use, this is recommended. When they are purchased for use in occupational therapy where there is little or no control over how and when they will be cleaned or whether they will be returned, medium-priced student grade brushes seem to be the most serviceable and the most economical. There are many kinds of brushes on the market and each artist soon learns which ones are the best for the type of work he does. Some painters have several brushes of one type and size to use in different colors and thereby save a great deal of wiping and cleaning as they paint. There are two common types of brushes used in oil painting:

(1) *Bristle brushes.* Bristle brushes (fig. 47) have rather stiff bristles. The most frequently

used in oil painting are the "brights" which are flat, thin brushes with short hair. The "flat" brush is also flat in shape, but the bristles are longer and thicker. The round bristle brush which comes to a point is used less frequently than the flat ones.

ROUND BRISTLE BRUSH

FLAT BRISTLE BRUSH – LONG HAIR – "FLAT"

FLAT BRISTLE BRUSH – SHORT HAIR – "BRIGHT"

Figure 47. Actual sizes of recommended bristle brushes.

POINTED ROUND SABLE BRUSH

FLAT "BRIGHT" SABLE BRUSH

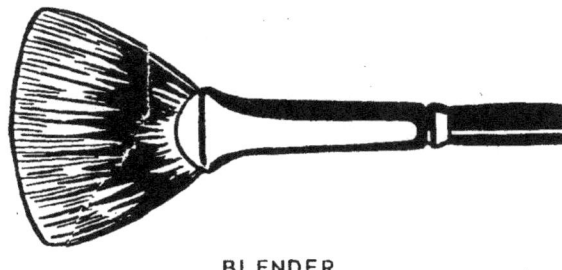

BLENDER

Figure 48. Actual sizes of recommended sable brushes.

(2) *Sable brushes.* Sable brushes are used for oil painting as well as for watercolors. They are made both flat and round (fig. 48). Although they are soft, they are somewhat springy and are useful in oil painting for fine detail, for soft brush strokes, and for delicate blending of colors.

(3) *Varnish brush.* A flat 1-inch varnish brush is used to put varnish on the painting. It is obtainable at any paint or hardware store and it does not need to be expensive.

(4) *Brush care.* Good brushes are expen-

SOLVENT SAVER BRUSH WASHER

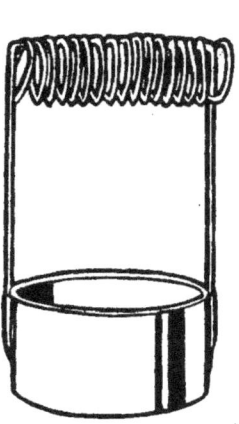

BRUSH WASHER WITH SPIRAL HOLDER FOR BRUSHES

Figure 49. Brush washers.

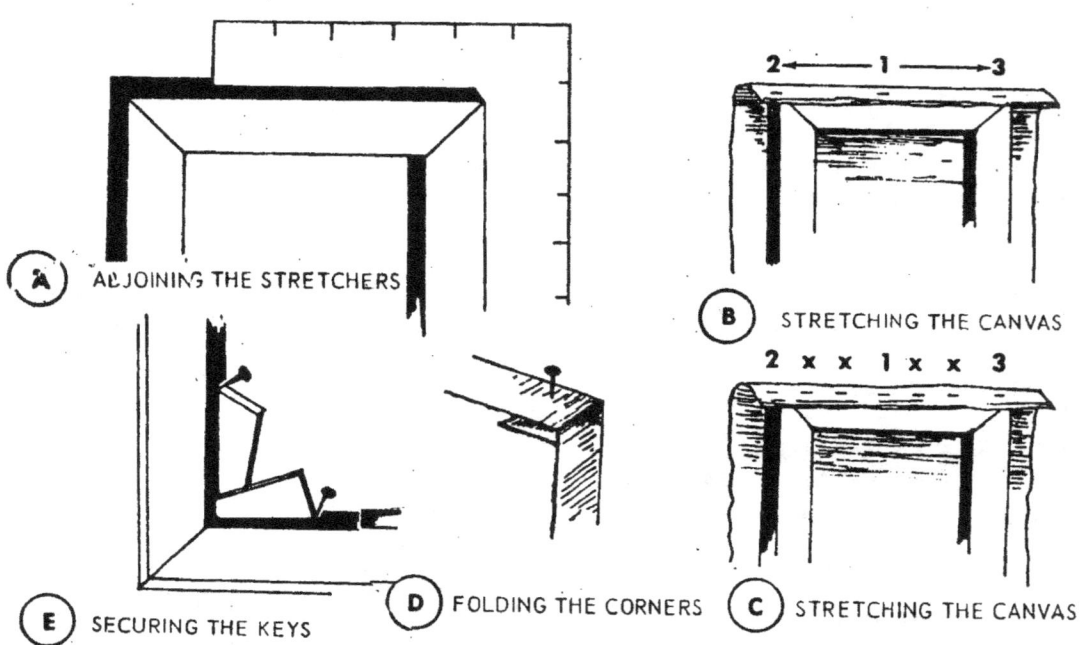

Figure 50. Stretching the canvas.

sive and they deserve good care. Paint should never be allowed to dry in a brush. To insure proper care, you should—

(a) *Rinse brush while working.* Rinse the brush in a solvent such as turpentine, kerosene, or mineral spirits and wipe it with a rag frequently as you work. The commercial washer in figure 49 keeps the brush above the dirty sediment which has settled in the bottom after other cleanings. It also keeps the solvent usable longer. This model can be made at home of two tin cans, with the smaller one cut to about an inch in height and then holes punched down into it. The other washer in figure 49 has a spring at the top which holds the brushes in the solvent when they are not being used.

(b) *Clean brushes after use.* After each painting session, insure that the brushes are well cleaned.

- *Paint out excess paint.* Paint out excess paint on newspaper, then rinse well in solvent, working the solvent up near the ferrule, the "heel" of the brush.
- *Wash brush.* Wash it with a mild face soap and in warm water. Work up a lather in the palm of the hand and rub the brush to clean it well. Rinse. Repeat this until the brush shows no trace of color.
- *Shape brush.* Rinse it again, then shape it carefully, and put it away to dry. Never stand a brush on the bristles.
- *Protect from moths.* If the brushes are to be stored over a period of time, take precautions against moths.

b. *Brush Washers.* These were discussed in a(4)(a) above.

b. *Canvas.* Canvases are available with different textures—rough, smooth, and medium. The selection is up to the artist, based on personal preference and the texture he wishes to have in the painting. Canvas sheets which come in tablet form are inexpensive and good for beginners. Canvas may be purchased already mounted on a rigid surface, or it may be purchased by the yard to be mounted by the artist. The latter method is less expensive and better because it does not warp, but it requires more preparation. The wooden stretchers to which the canvas is usually fastened can be patented strips which are purchased with their corners already mortised and tenoned. Four strips can be assembled to form a rectangular frame of any desired dimension. When the frame is assembled, the canvas is cut to a size 1 inch larger all around than the stretcher (12 by 14 inches for a 10- by 12-inch stretcher). A carpenter's square should be used to check to see if the stretcher strips are correctly alined (A, fig. 50). If the stretcher joints are loose, submersion in water will swell the wood and immobilize the joints for some time. Then the canvas is placed on the stretcher, with its face toward the artist, using these steps—

(1) Fasten the canvas on the middle of a stretcher strip with an upholstery tack 3/8 inch long. Pull the canvas in direction 2, (B, fig. 50), and place the second tack near the end of a stretcher strip.

(2) Next pull the canvas in direction 3, (B, fig. 50), and place the third tack near the opposite end of the stretcher strip.

(3) Fasten the canvas with the remaining tacks placed about 2 inches apart as in C, figure 50. Each tack on the illustration is marked with an "X."

(4) Repeat steps 1–3 on the opposite side of the stretcher strip; then on the two remaining strips.

(5) Fold the canvas as shown in D, figure 50. Place the keys (small wooded wedges that come with the stretchers) in the grooves on each stretcher strip and hammer them in carefully.

To hold the keys in place, drive a nail in front of each (E, fig. 50).

NOTE

When the work is completed, the canvas should be smooth and taut, but it should not be overstrained.

d. Charcoal. Charcoal (sec. II) is used to sketch in spacing and ideas before painting.

e. Easel. Because different types and models of easels are being developed (fig. 51), it is wise to look carefully at what is available before one is purchased. If working outdoors is contemplated the easel should be lightweight, folding, and sturdy; the hardware should be rustproof; and the legs should be pointed. Easels of aluminum have been used quite satisfactorily in the past few years. There are many designs; the choice is up to the artist, based on the type of work he does.

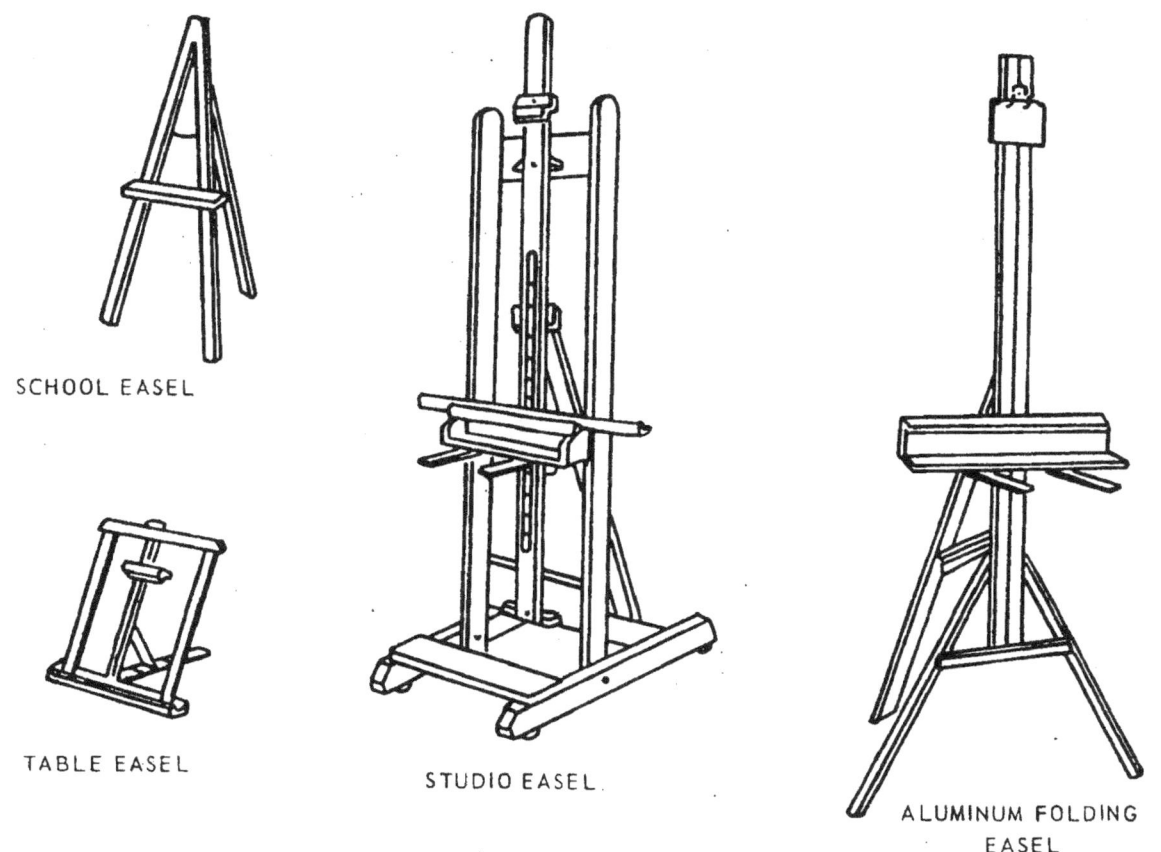

Figure 51. Types of easels.

f. Paint. In this work, there is no substitute for good quality paint. Not only does good paint look better, but the manner in which it responds enables the artist to do better work and derive more satisfaction from his work. In addition to the conventional oil paint, an acrylic polymer, resin-based paint will also be considered because of its facility for work with patients.

(1) *Oil base color.* Oil colors are made by mixing pigments (dry colored powders) with a high grade linseed oil. The pigments do not dissolve in the oil, but powerful mechanical grinding disperses them uniformly throughout the oil. Oil paint has a thick creamy consistency as it comes out of the tube. If not altered with a painting medium, it will retain the brush marks when dry. The drying time of oil paints is influenced by the type of paint, the color, the medium used, the thickness of the paint, and the atmospheric conditions. At least a day is required for some, and a week may be required for others.

- Oil colors are put in tubes of different sizes and are sold by the box (table 1). The smaller tubes (II or IV) are usually the most economical to buy for use in occupational therapy. However, white is used more than any other one color, so it is usually purchased in larger tubes.
- There are some 70 oil colors on the market. The colors selected depend, in a large measure, not only on the ones with which the artist likes to work, but also upon the subject matter. Here is a list of colors suggested for a basic landscape pallet:

Alizarin crimson
Burnt sienna
Cadmium red light
Cadmium yellow light
French ultramarine
Ivory black
Light red
Viridian
Yellow ochre
Zinc or Titanium white

Table 1. Tube Sizes and Quantity in a Box

Tube No.	Size	Number in each box
II	½" x 2"	6
IV	½" x 4"	6
VI	¾" x 3⅛"—Economy size	6
IX	1" x 4"—Studio tube 1.25 oz	3
X	1" x 6"	3
XI	1½" x 6"	1

They can be supplemented at a later time by the following:
Burnt umber
Cadmium orange
Cadmium yellow deep
Cerulean blue
Cobalt blue
Oxide of chromium opaque
Raw sienna

(2) *Acrylic polymer resin paint.* These synthetic paints have become a widely used fine arts medium in the last decade. There are several reasons why they should be considered for use in occupational therapy. Perhaps the most important reason for occupational therapists is that they are water thinned, thereby eliminating the need for turpentine and other painting mediums. Brushes can be cleaned easily in water—but it must be done immediately. They are cheaper than oils and less messy. The paint dries as fast as water does, which is a boon in some ways to the impatient amateur painter. This one paint can be used for a variety of fine arts and craft techniques. It is available in 1 1/8-inch by 5-inch and in 1 1/2-inch by 6 1/4-inch tubes in over 30 colors and at a lower cost than fine oils.

g. Paint Rags. Rags may be obtained from any source. They should be free from loose lint and be absorbent.

h. Palette. Paint is kept ready for the artist and is mixed on the palette (A, fig. 52). Some artists prefer a wood palette; others, plastic. The disposable paper palettes have been found quite satisfactory and time-saving in a setting such as is found in occupational therapy. They come in pads of 50 sheets of oilproof, waterproof papers, each of which is torn off of the pad and then destroyed.

i. Palette Cups. These small cups (B, fig. 52) slip over the edge of the palette and hold the mixing medium such as oil and turpentine.

j. Palette Knives. There are many types of palette knives (fig. 53). Some are for mixing colors on the palette and some are used as a brush in painting. The selection is based on the intended use and the preference of the artist.

k. Painting Mediums. A painting medium is any of several liquids used with oil paints to accelerate or to retard the drying time of the paint. It is wise to use these sparingly as they alter the quality of the paint.

(1) *Turpentine.* "Turp" is probably the most

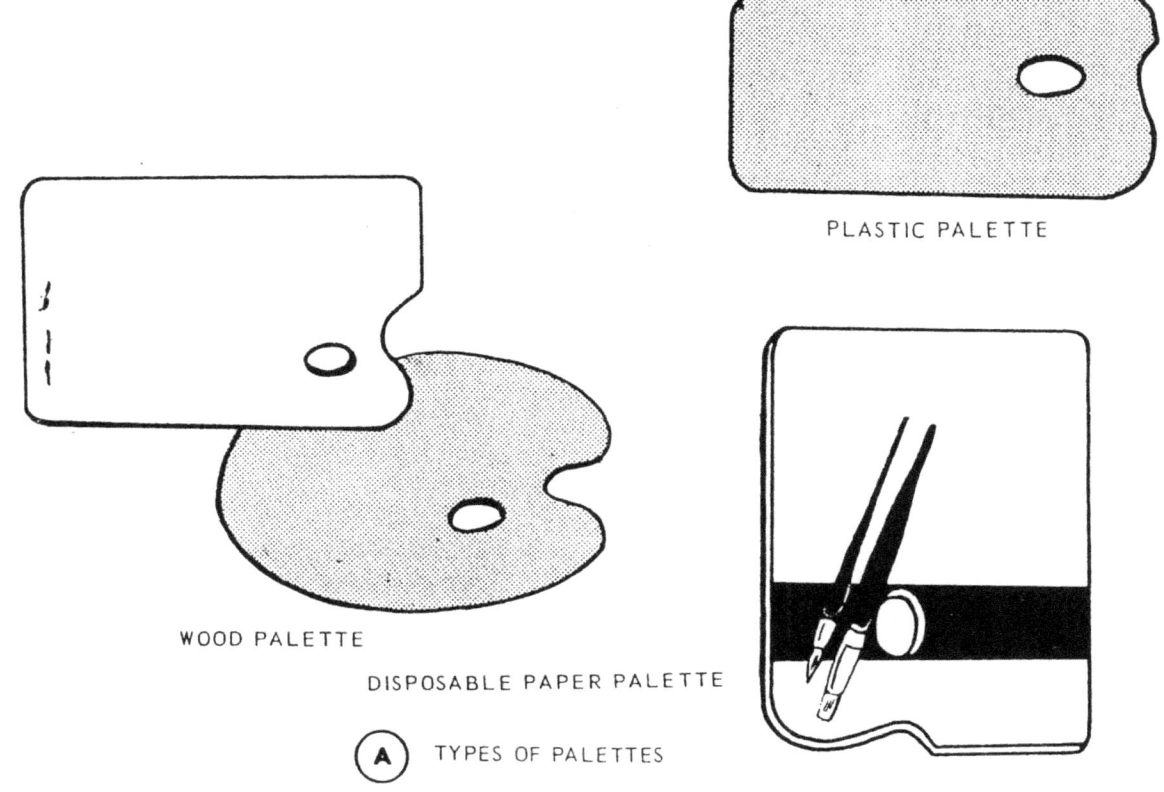

Figure 52Ⓐ. Types of palettes and palette cups.

Figure 52Ⓑ. Types of palettes and palette cups.

frequently used medium to cut the consistency of the paint and to speed drying time. Only the pure gum spirits or rectified turpentine should be used. It is available at artist's supply stores rather than at hardware stores.

(2) *Cobalt dryer.* Small amounts added to the paint speed drying time; too much dryer affects the permanence of the paint.

(3) *Linseed oil.* The addition of linseed oil to the paint slows drying time. Too much will make the paint stick and it will yellow after the paint dries.

(4) *Stand oil.* This slows drying time and is also non-yellowing.

(5) *Mixed medium.* To obtain a medium which will give the desired texture and qualities to the paint, several of the media above may be mixed. Some artists prefer a formula of their own; others purchase a mixture already mixed. Some favorite formulas are as follows:
    (a) 1/3 capal oil varnish
        1/3 linseed oil
        1/3 turpentine
    (b) 1/2 turpentine
        1/2 linseed oil
    (c) Oil of capal
        Stand oil
        Linseed oil

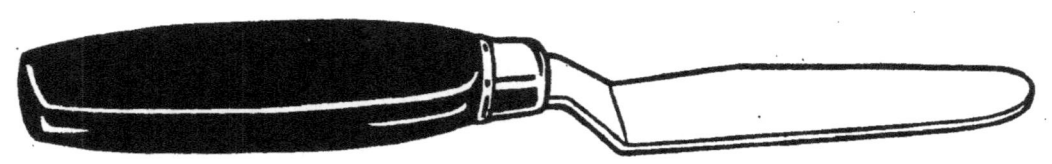

TROWEL SHAPED PALETTE KNIFE

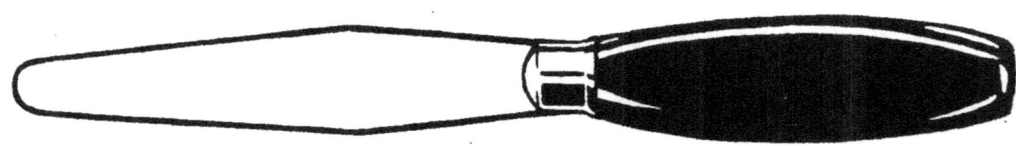

STRAIGHT BLADE PALETTE KNIFE

Figure 53. Palette knives.

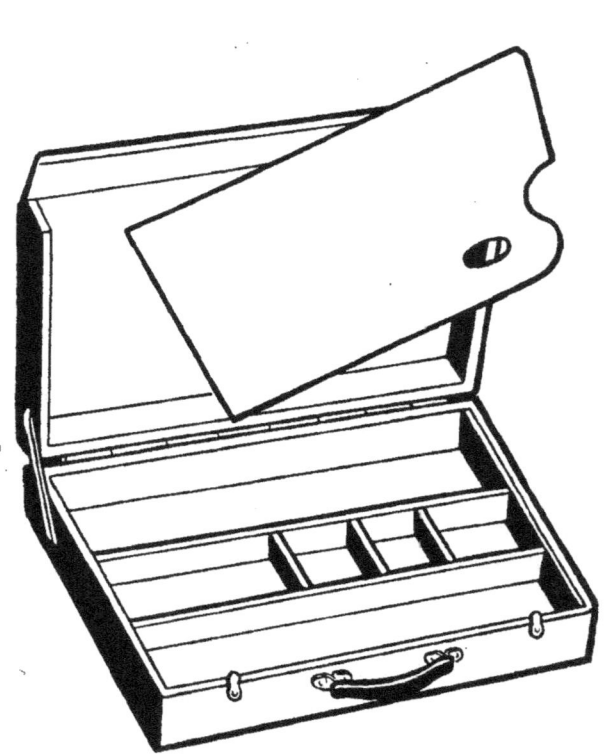

Figure 54. Sketch box.

l. Sketch Box. This is another item which is selected according to the needs and the preferences of the artist. There are many types, filled and empty, with different types of palettes, different sizes, partitions, and materials. Some are basic, others have a number of extra features. Figure 54 shows a portable sketch box. Some come equipped with detachable legs.

m. Painting Stool. Some artists would rather stand while they work; others like to sit down, at least some of the time. A folding stool is handy to put the sketch box on, if not to sit on.

16. Processes

a. Set the Palette. Setting the palette (putting the paint on the palette) is an individual matter. Each artist has his own way—no way is right or wrong. There are some considerations, however, to take into account when a personal method is developed.

(1) Once a handy and comfortable arrangement of paint on the palette has been found, it should be kept consistent so that having a certain hue in a certain place is automatic and no time is wasted looking for it.

(2) Some artists follow the spectrum found in the color wheel when setting up their palette.

(3) Putting side by side the colors which are mixed most frequently is another way to plan a palette.

(4) The time to clean the paint from the palette is also at the discretion of the artist. Some clean it after each use, while others let the paint accumulate until the surface is too full of paint to use and then they clean it.

b. Try Out Brushes. Before a picture is started, practice with various brushes and palette knives on a piece of scrap to see how they respond and what they will do. Make thin lines and wide lines; paint in an area with different strokes for different effects. Try first with pure color as it comes from the tube.

c. Try Mixing Paint. Next, try mixing the colors to see how they respond. Mixing colors is an art and a skill based on understanding of the principles involved and experience. Paragraph 3a(7) gives a basic theory of mixing colors. For additional information, consult a book on oil painting. After working out step (*b*) above and this step and obtaining some familiarity with the brushes and paint, the beginning painter can then think about painting.

d. Decide What to Paint. The key thought here is to keep it simple. Do not try to paint all that is seen—paint only a small area of it and leave out the details. Outdoors, a tree or a door may be selected. Indoors, a simple still life may be the answer.

e. Sketch in Forms. Roughly sketch the picture over the entire canvas with charcoal. This is just to get the size and placement of the objects. Go over these charcoal lines with a very thin solution of black paint so that the charcoal can be rubbed off. If it is left on, it will "muddy" the color.

f. Paint. Painting should be done in the most comfortable way for each artist. Some hold the brush near the ferrule, some out toward the center. Some people sit, some stand, some hold the palette, some would rather have it on the table. Following, though, are a few suggestions which may be of some help:

(1) A painter should step away occasionally to view the work. This will help to keep the beginner from falling into the trap of overdeveloping one small area, thereby losing the breadth of effect or the meaning of the total picture. Work on the entire canvas as a unit.

(2) Many errors can be corrected by painting over. If, however, in working with an area, it becomes hopeless, scrape off the paint from that area with a palette knife, rub the area with a rag, and start over. Now it is possible to profit from the mistakes made in the first attempt.

(3) It is often helpful for the beginning painter to paint some objects which are distasteful, rather than pleasant, with regard to his taste for subject matter. The task of painting a distasteful subject in itself offers a challenge to the artist and may help to develop a critical eye and more awareness in the artist.

(4) When painting out of doors or when painting natural scenes, it is more realistic to use tints, shades, and subtlety in color rather than brilliant color or color directly from the tube.

(5) A three-dimensional quality can be developed in the painting by using highlights and shadows and by overlapping tints and shades, rather than using dark outlines which are often overworked and tend to hold the picture together.

(6) Perfection should not be the target in painting, but rather enjoyment of the experience with paint. Be patient; skills will develop with practice. Keep your paintings for your own evaluation and constructive criticism from friends.

(7) Plenty of old rags should be kept on hand for cleaning up and for removing paint from wrong areas. Do not paint in your best clothes unless they are well protected by an outer garment such as a smock or an old shirt.

(8) If the tops of the tubes are difficult to unscrew, they may be loosened by heating them with a match. A box of matches should be a part of the artist's equipment.

17. Safety Precautions

a. Certain colors of oil paint contain copper arsenate or lead, which makes them poisonous in varying degrees. Because of this, precautions must be taken with some types of patients to insure that paint is not ingested.

b. In a psychiatric clinic, it is wise to keep such items as turpentine and spirits in small containers rather than in the usual quart or gallon sizes. Thus, if a patient ingests some, it will be a sublethal amount and treatment can be effective.

18. Therapeutic Aspects of Oil Painting

a. Physically Disabled Patients. Oils can be used to some degree in the treatment of patients with physical disabilities. Painting can be used as prewriting experience for patients with injured hands. It can be used quite effectively with upper extremity amputees as a means of gaining control of the prosthesis and obtaining confidence in its use.

b. Psychiatric Patients. Oil painting is used

very effectively in occupational therapy as a mean of expression for psychiatric patients. The choice of color and subject matter may give important clues as to what the patient is thinking and how he feels. Oil paint stays workable long enough for the patient to be able to work without feeling the pressure of the medium as he would with watercolor, for instance. Several days later the patient can repaint an area as his feelings change.

changes made by the patient may reflect the effects of his therapy and his recent encounters and experiences. Any important comment should be reported to the psychiatrist.

c. General Medical and Surgical Patients. Long-term, medical-surgical patients can profit greatly from the development of interest and skill in this ever-challenging hobby.

Section V. STENCILING

19. General

a. Stenciling is an ancient process, having been known by the Egyptians as early as 2400 B.C. Today it is a simple, adaptable craft which can be used when a design is to be repeated several times.

b. A stencil is a sheet of thin but strong material from which shapes have been cut so that when it is laid on a surface and color applied, a certain figure is produced.

c. Stenciling may be used for decorating greeting cards, stationery, note paper, posters, place mats, luncheon sets, scarves, chairs, toys, and wastebaskets, to name just a few.

20. Tools, Equipment, and Supplies

a. Brushes. Stencil brushes have short, rather thick handles. The bristles are set into a round ferrule and are cut flat at the end, rather than tapered to a point. They are available in several sizes. The selection used depends upon the size of the work being done.

b. Drawing Board. A drawing board with a smooth surface is important.

c. Knife. To cut paper stencils, a thin, sharp knife is essential. A stencil knife is ideal, as is an X-acto knife with a suitable balde (fig. 56). If a sharp knife is not available, a new, single-edged razor blade is a good substitute. It is tiring

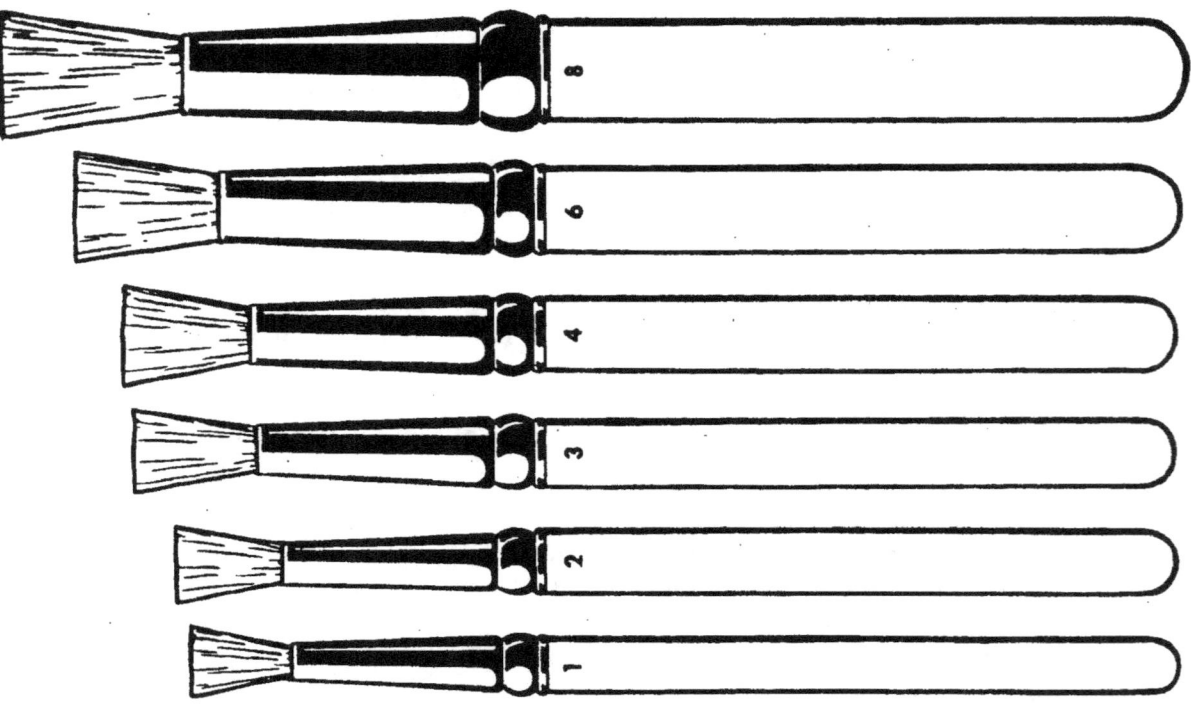

Figure 55. Stencil brushes.

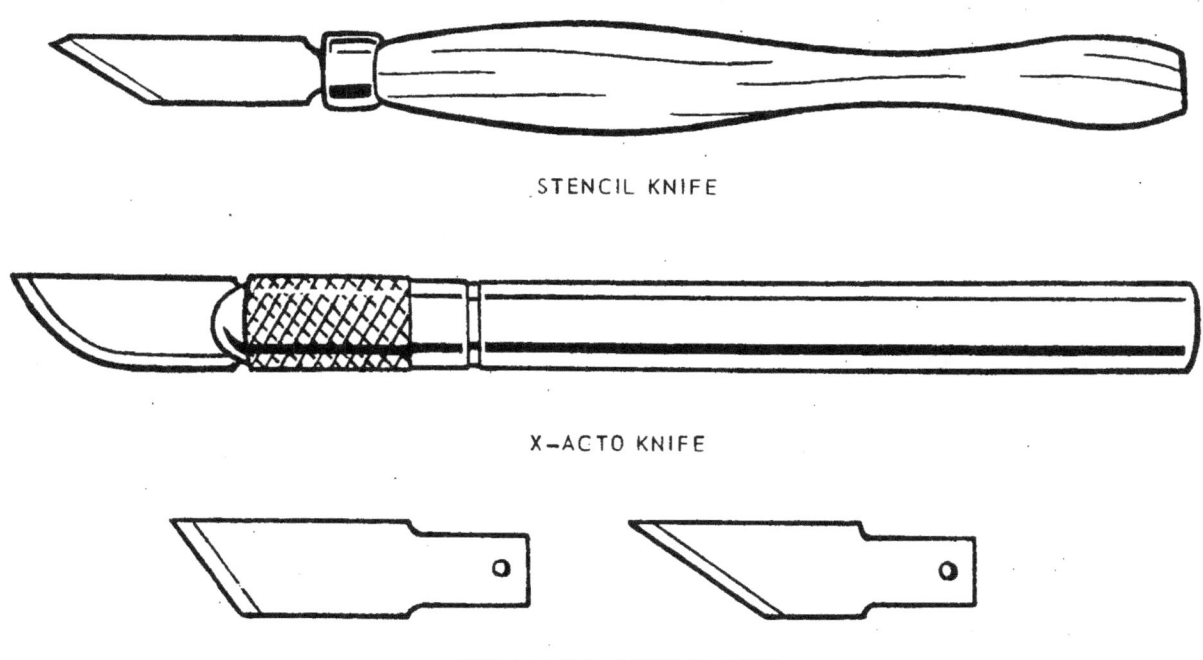

Figure 56. Knives for cutting stencils.

on the hand, however, if a great deal of cutting is to be done.

d. Material to Stencil. Any smooth surface that will take paint can be stenciled, to include the following suggested materials:

(1) Fabric, such as cotton, linen, rayon, silk, or synthetic fibers which will absorb paint. The fabric should have a smooth weave and should not be fuzzy.

(2) Glass.
(3) Metal.
(4) Paper.
(5) Plastic.
(6) Wood.

e. Pallet. A pallet tray (opaque white trays with depressions) may be used for small amounts of color. For larger amounts, a tile or a piece of glass or plexiglass may be substituted.

f. Pallet Knife. Pallet knives (fig. 53) are best for mixing certain types of paint.

g. Paint. The type of paint used depends upon the material used.

(1) Fabric. Textile paint with *extender* to make the paint go farther and *thinner* to thin the paint.

(2) Glass, metal, plastic, wood. Oil paint.

(3) Paper. Watercolor, tempera, or ink.

h. Ruler. A ruler is helpful.

i. Stencil Paper. Several commercial stencil papers of different weights are available on the market. There are also some substitutes for commercial stencil paper which are very satisfactory (3 below).

(1) *Stencil board.* Commercial stencil board is a heavyweight, tough paper which is impervious to water and oil. This material is ideal because it holds up well and, when cut, has clean, sharp edges. It is relatively expensive, however, and is not always available in an occupational therapy clinic.

(2) *Stencil paper.* A strong, transparent, moisture-resistant paper which cuts easily and holds its edge.

(3) *Substitutes.* Substitutes with some of these same qualities include exposed X-ray film, tympan paper, and acetate paper.

j. Square. Include a square with equipment.

k. Tracing Paper. This is for tracing the parts of the design from which the stencil is made.

21. Process

Unless readymade stencils are used, the design must be selected, then colored, and the stencil cut before any actual painting can be started.

a. Select a Design. Usually each color in the design requires a separate stencil, which can make stenciling with a number of colors quite complex. As in any new undertaking, it is wise to start with a simple, two-color design (fig. 57).

Figure 57. Color design.

(1) Select the design and colors.

(2) Line a rectangle around the drawing to serve as a locator for the stencils as they are made.

b. Trace the Design.

(1) On a sheet of tracing paper, trace all of the areas that are to be the same color. In the corner of the tracing, mark the right angle of at least two corners of the rectangle around the design. Thees are registry angles (fig. 58).

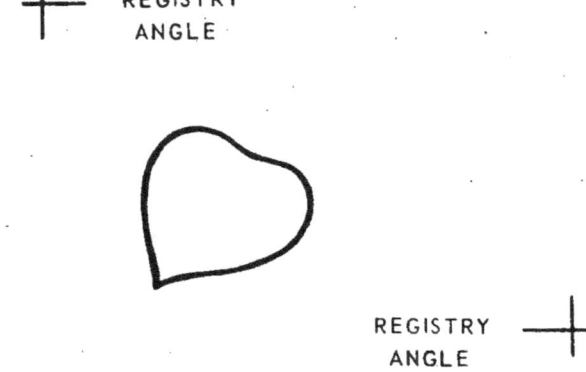

Figure 58. Stencil No. 1.

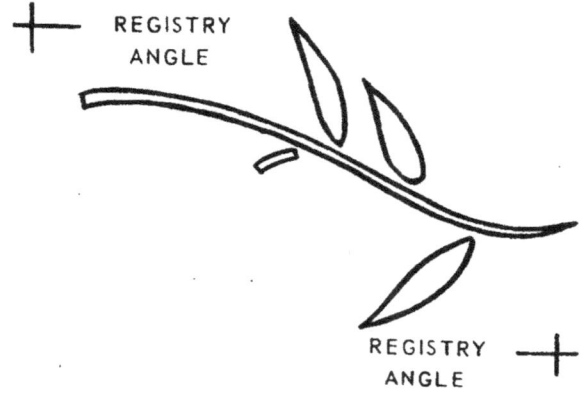

Figure 59. Stencil No. 2.

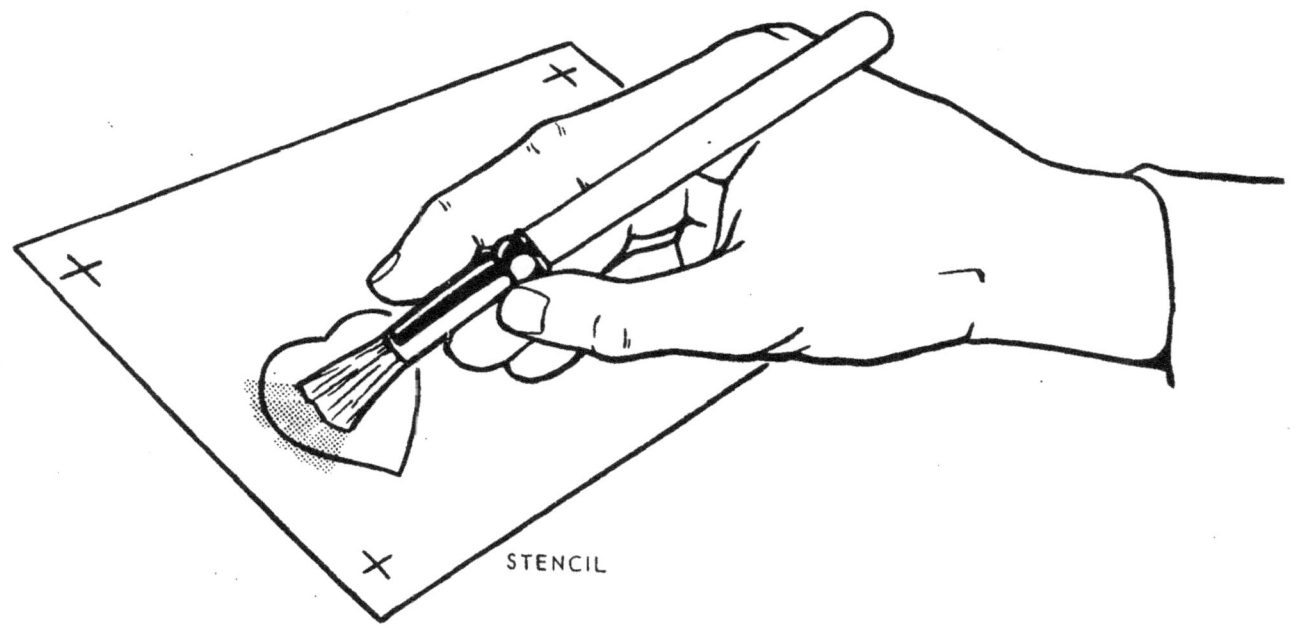

Figure 60. Stroking.

(2) Retrace each drawing on stencil paper, using a different sheet of paper for each color. The tracing must include the registry angles.

(3) Repeat steps (1) and (2) above, for each color in the design (fig. 59).

c. Cut the Stencil. After the tracings have been made on stencil paper, cut the stencil. To do this, lay the stencil paper on a sheet of Masonite or heavy cardboard and with a sharp knife or a razor blade, cut out the traced areas. The cut lines of the stencil paper must be sharp.

d. Prepare the Background.

NOTE
Steps (1) and (2) below are not used for material other than fabric.

(1) If a washable fabric is being used as background, remove the sizing by washing the material in lukewarm water and mild suds. It must then be dried and ironed.

(2) Next, stretch the fabric over a firm backing such as the drawing board and hold securely with tacks or with tape.

(3) Decide exactly where the design will be on the background paper, cloth, metal, or wood, and mark registry angles. This can be marked with removable ink or paint, pins, thread, or paper.

e. Paint the Stencil.

(1) Select the stencil for the lightest coler first (fig. 58) and place the corner of the stencil paper accurately in the registry mark on the background material. Tack the stencil in place.

(2) Get some paint on the stencil brush, then brush or wipe it nearly dry on a paper towel. If there is too much paint in the brush, it will smear the background.

(3) With the brush held in nearly vertical position, stroke lightly over the opening of the stencil from the outside edge toward the center of the background material (fig. 60).

(4) Carefully pull the stencil back from time to time to see how much paint is being deposited on the background material. It is frequently darker than it appears to be.

(5) Shade by stroking more in the area to be darker.

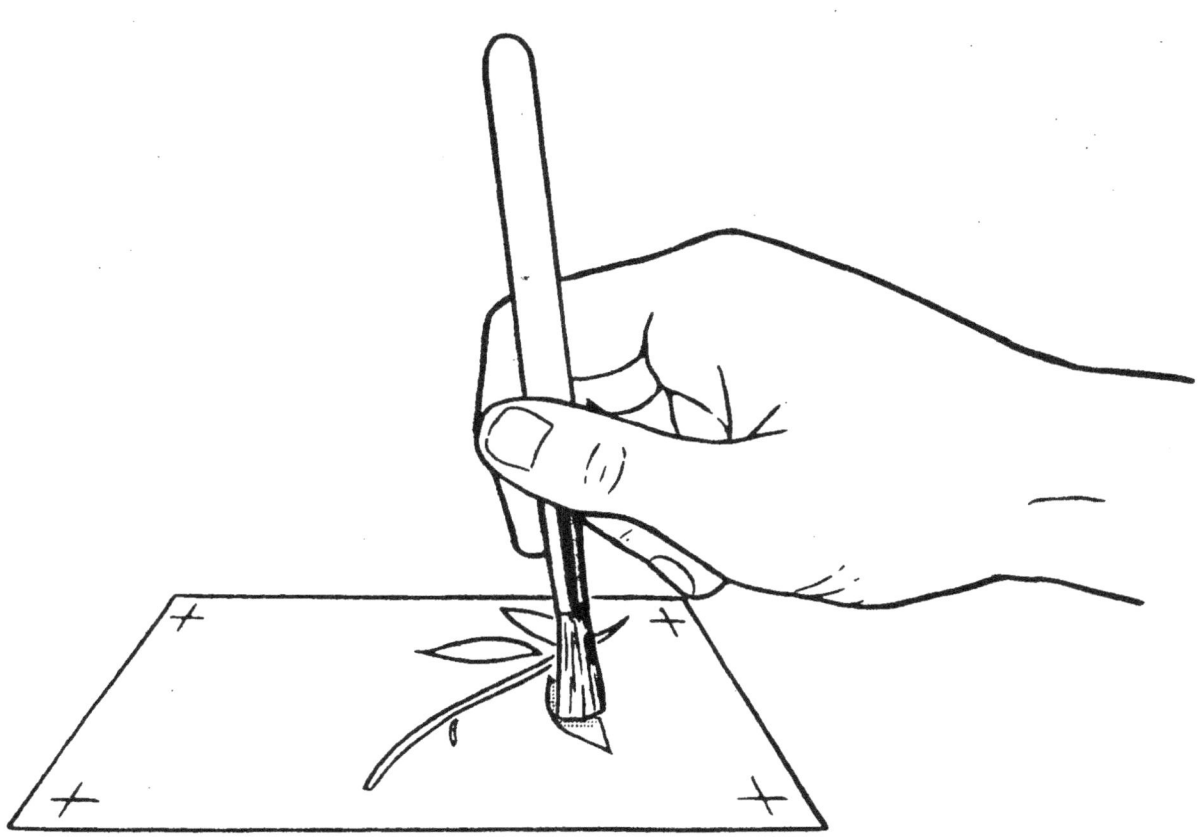

Figure 61. Stippling.

(6) To obtain a rounded appearance to the design, make the outer edges of the design darker.

(7) Usually, stroke so as to conform to the direction of the plane being painted.

(8) Use variations if needed. *For example,* it is also possible to hold the brush perpendicular to the stencil and stipple the color on. This is the way to color small areas that are too small to stroke (fig. 61). Spattering the color is also an interesting variation. It is especially appropriate to spatter ink on paper. The use of both the positive and the negative parts of the stencil can provide additional variations in stenciling. The positive stencil (A, fig. 62) makes a colored figure on the background while the negative stencil (B, fig. 62) makes a white figure on a colored background.

f. Set the Color in Cloth. Allow the textile paint to dry for 24 hours, then press the design on the wrong side with a hot iron. Use an iron set to the temperature which corresponds to the background fabric.

g. Correct Mistakes on Cloth. If the cloth is large, many accidents with paint can be prevented by covering the area around the stencil with paper. If a paint spot must be removed near the design, rub the spot carefully with penetrator thinner. If the paint spot is away from the design, rub in extender, let it stand for a few minutes, then wash the area carefully with soap and cold water.

22. Design

This medium lends itself to decoration, abstraction, and design, rather than to naturalism. Designs should have well-defined areas, especially for the beginner. As skill develops, more color may be added, along with more intricacy of design. The design must allow for each "hole" to be surrounded by enough stencil paper to hold securely enough to work over it. For instance, a design for the letter "O" must provide some means of support for the inner circle of stencil paper (fig. 63).

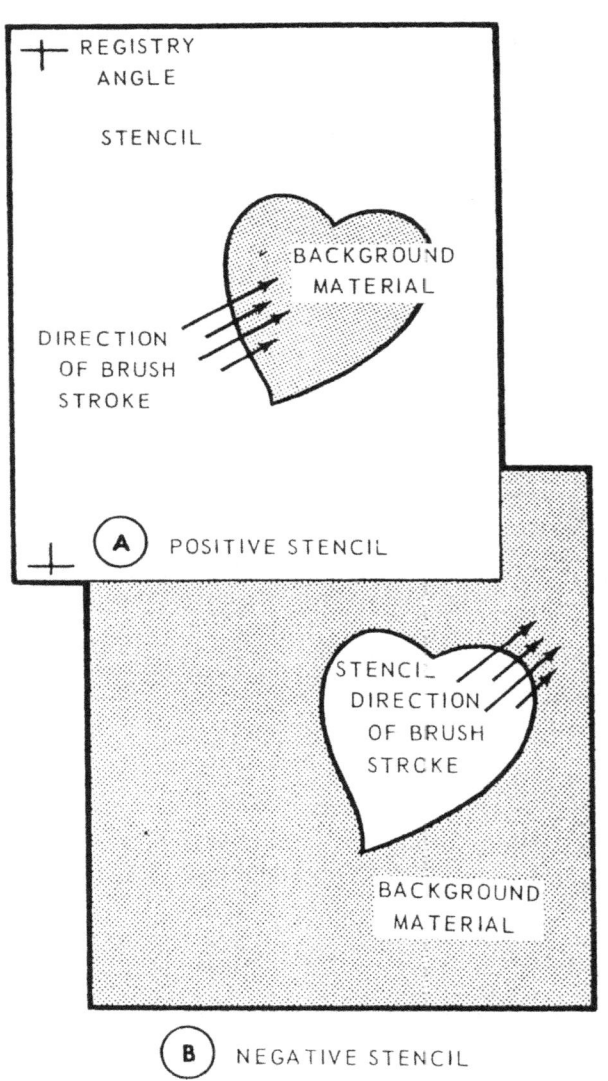

Figure 62. Use of positive and negative stencils.

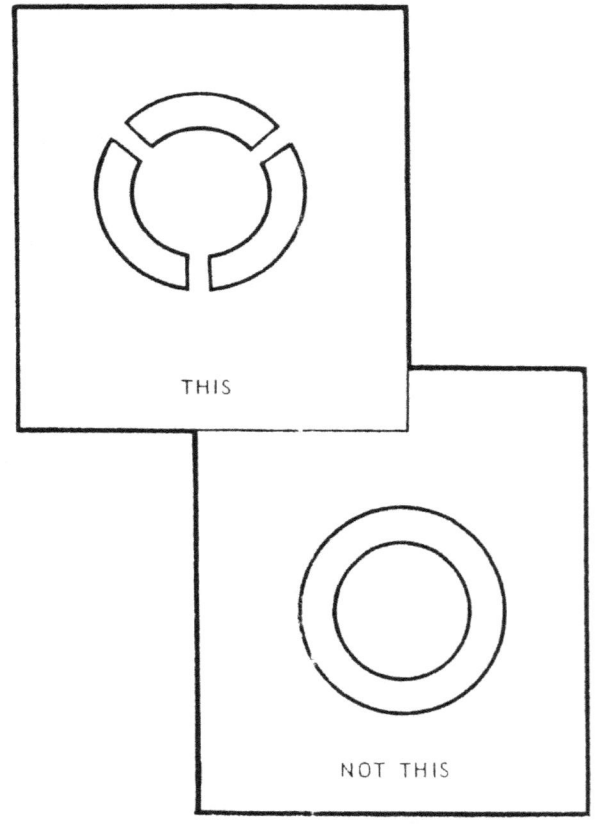

Figure 63. Stencil for the letter "O."

23. Therapeutic Aspects

a. Physically Disabled Patients. Some therapy is derived from handling the brush while painting. Beginning wrist flexion and extension is obtained while stippling. It may be felt that preparation for this work is too time-consuming for the amount of therapy involved unless the patient is not interested in other forms of the same exercise.

b. Psychiatric Patients. Stenciling is unusually adaptable to the needs of the patients.

(1) If a precut stencil is used and the colors are predetermined, stencil painting can be a highly structured activity. Developing the design and color and then planning and making the stencils can be a creative, absorbing task.

(2) Stenciling can be a short-term project or it can be very long term and involved.

(3) In a structured setup, a successful picture is almost guaranteed, but a complex, creative effort is highly subject to errors.

c. General Medical and Surgical Patients. The gradability of the complexity of painting is adaptable to the needs and limitations of these patients. Female patients are usually more interested in stenciling than male patients.

Section VI. WATERCOLOR

24. General

a. Watercolor is a light, flowing paint which should be applied spontaneously. It is a difficult medium to use because of the speed which must be employed to complete the work while the painting is still wet, and because it is almost impossible to correct errors. Its advantages are that the paint is relatively inexpensive, may be stored in a small area, and is easy to clean up because it is water soluble.

b. Watercolors are classified into two general groups: transparent and opaque. Both types are often used to paint landscapes or still life drawings, though any subject may be chosen. In making signs and posters, the poster paints (opaque) are especially appropriate.

(1) *Transparent watercolors.* Transparent paints allow the white of the paper to show through, giving a fresh, light feeling to the painting. However, this transparency makes it nearly impossible to cover mistakes.

(2) *Opaque watercolor.* Unlike transparent watercolor, the opaque is not affected by the underlying color and thus is more easily handled by the beginner who may wish to cover mistakes. If the opaque paints are used without thinning, a rich texture may be achieved; however, they may also be thinned if more of the feeling of the transparent washes is desired. This thinned opaque paint does not attain as fresh a feeling as the transparent.

25. Tools, Equipment, and Supplies

a. Brushes. The selection of brushes in figure 64 has been recommended for watercolor painting. This great a selection is not at all necessary, however. The No. 3, No. 6, and the 3/4-inch brushes are all that are needed for the work usually done in occupational therapy. The 3/4-inch brush is a work brush for large areas such as sky. The usually valid theory that it is economical to purchase the best brushes available does not apply where brushes are easily lost and are not always left perfectly clean. Medium-priced brushes are usually the most satisfactory and economical under such circumstances. Care in storing brushes by wrapping them in paper keeps the bristles in shape and free from dust.

b. Drawing Board. A drawing board with a smooth surface is needed.

c. Eraser, Art Gum. This eraser is made from pure gum rubber and is used for safe and quick cleaning of artwork.

d. Opaque Watercolors. Opaque watercolors are available in several forms, including egg tempera, casine, acrylic, and poster paints. Only the more commonly available poster paints, commonly termed "tempera," are discussed here. These opaque watercolors are available in ready-mixed form or in powder form. The ready-mixed form saves the chore of mixing, but it will dry out if not used. It is available in sets or by the jar. The powder form stores without damage over a period of time. It is sold in 1-pound cans. Recommended colors are as follows:

Black	Green	Red
Blue	Orange	White
Brown	Purple	Yellow

e. Transparent Watercolors. Transparent watercolor paint is available in two forms—

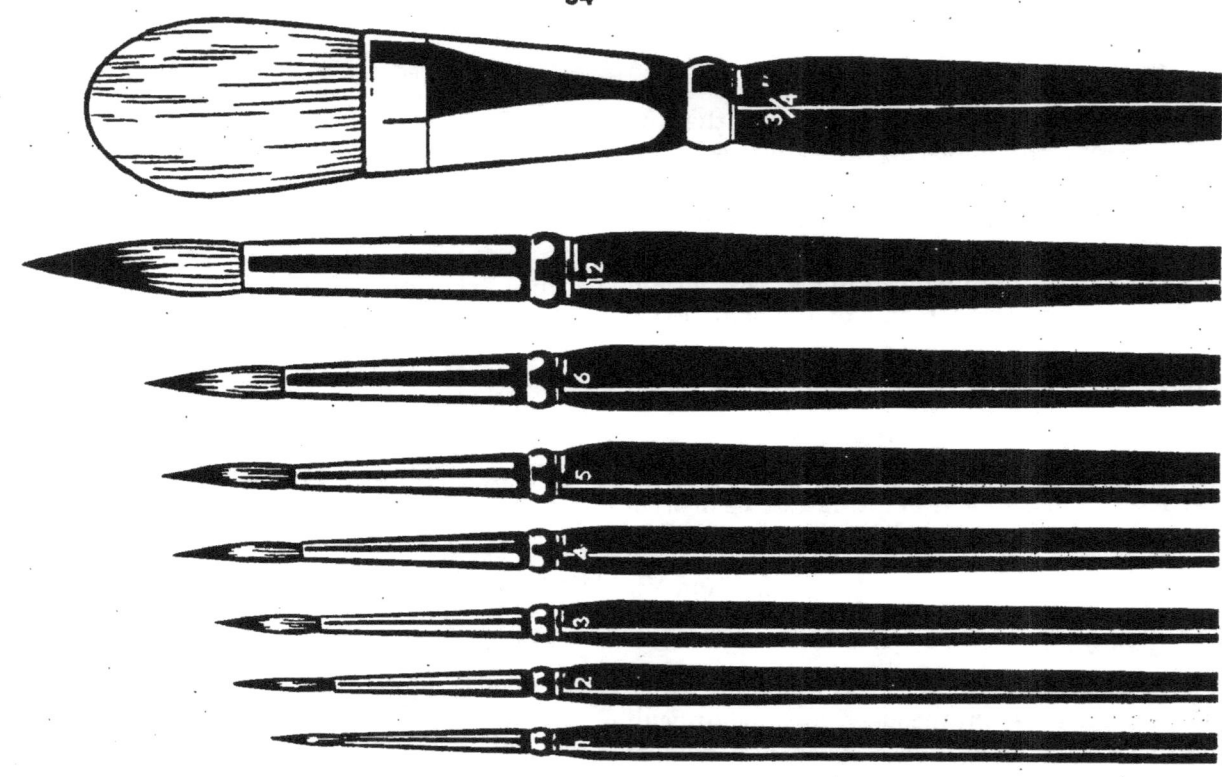

Figure 64. Watercolor brushes.

(1) *Watercolor tubes.* Watercolor paint comes in tubes. It can be purchased in sets or by the single tube. Because the paint has a water base, it dries quite rapidly unless the cap is kept tightly closed. The following list are colors which are recommended for starting:

Alizarin crimson	Ivory black
Burnt sienna	Lemon yellow
Cadmium red	Monastral blue
Ultramarine blue	Yellow ochre
Veridian	

(2) *Semimoist watercolor.* These sets are available in different sizes. The half-pan in figure 65 has 8 colors: the whole pan has 16. This is a convenient way to take watercolors to the ward. It is also easy for the patients to handle. Replacement pans are available for any of the colors, but they are usually sold by the dozen.

Figure 65. Semimoist watercolor paint set.

f. Pallet Tray. These are opaque white trays with depressions designed for mixing colors. A smaller but similar tray is made into the lid of the semimoist watercolor box.

g. Paper. Watercolor paper is available in different grades, textures, sizes, and prices. It can be purchased by the sheet or in tablets. The budget, the type, and the number of patients, as well as personal preference, are considered when slection is made. A durable paper which is made to resist wrinkles even after it is wet should be used. It is good to have a selection of cold press paper, which is suitable for large free paintings, and hot press paper, which is smoother and is used for more detailed work. However, a rough paper is better for transparent watercolors. If large sheets of paper are purchased, they can be halved or quartered to provide the best size for the patient. Paper must be stored out flat, however, rather than rolled. Illustration board is usually used with opaque paint for such things as posters and signs.

h. Tape, 2-Inch, Gummed. This is used to hold the paper on the board while it is drying.

i. Sponge, Elephant Ear. This soft sponge is sometimes used to put wash on large areas.

j. Water Jar. Any jars will do to hold water for cleaning and rinsing out brushes.

26. Using Transparent Watercolor

a. Stretching Paper. All papers except the very heavy 300- and 400-pound papers must be stretched before painting. This stretching prevents uneven wrinkling and buckling of the paper.

(1) *Preparing watercolor paper.*

(a) Soak the paper in water for 1–3 minutes.

(b) Lift one side of the paper by its corners and allow the water to drain.

(c) Lay the paper flat on the drawing board so that no air bubbles form beneath the paper.

(d) Blot off the excess water with a clean rag or sponge.

(e) Tape the paper tightly on the drawing board, with four strips of gummed tape, each strip 2 inches longer than the sides of the paper.

(f) Allow the paper to dry as it is taped to the board.

(2) *Preparing illustration board.*

(a) Moisten both sides of the board with a sponge.

(b) Place the board on a clean, hard surface under weights.

(c) Allow the board to dry.

b. Transparent Watercolor Painting. Choose simple subjects for this type of painting. Start over again if the work does not go as it should. Some corrections can be made, but do not lose the brilliance of white paper. An interesting additional technique is the use of pen and ink applied over a watercolor wash to outline or accent figures.

(1) Sketch the subject lightly in outline on prepared paper.

(2) Wet the paper and paint onto it before it dries if a soft blended effect is desired. To obtain sharper lines, use drier paper.

(3) Dip brush in water and mix pool of color as needed on pallet. Test the color on a piece of scrap paper before using. Add more water to lighten the value.

(4) Begin painting by flowing on light colors first, using 3/4-inch flat scale brush or elephant ear sponge for washing in large areas. Use color generously, keeping light areas warm (yellow, red, orange, and brown) and shadows cool (green, blue, purple).

(5) Apply the intermediate values next over the dry or damp underpainting.

(6) Apply dark values, outlines, and accents last. Use a No. 12 round sable brush for shadows and small areas.

c. Framing the Picture. In framing a watercolor, the picture is covered with glass to protect the surface from dust and dirt. Watercolors sent to exhibititions must be framed and under glass. In framing, a mat to surround the picture is cut from a strong mat board. The mat may be white or may be painted a discreet neutral tint. A large margin of 4 to 5 inches should be allowed on an average-size painting, though a narrower mat will look better if the frame is to be wide. The mat should be about 1/2 inch wider on the bottom than on the sides or top. The frame may measure from 1 to 4 inches wide, depending on the size and nature of the picture. The wood may be waxed, stained, or painted.

27. Opaque Watercolors—Poster Paints

a. Sketch the subject lightly on heavy paper or illustration board.

b. Follow the instructions for transparent watercolors, but remember that the paint is opaque, so it is not affected by the underlying surface in the same manner as the transparent.

c. Use white paint to lighten the color value, though a semitransparent wash may be made by adding water to the opaque paint.

d. Achieve texture through the application of several layers of paint or by the addition of ingredients such as sand or asbestos.

28. Therapeutic Aspects

a. Physically Disabled Patients. In physical disabilities, watercolor painting may provide prewriting activity or may be used to increase the dexterity of the hand.

b. Psychiatric Patients. This medium provides a means of self-expression for the patient and it may give the psychiatrist opportunity to gain further insight into the patient's condition.

c. General Medical and Surgical Patients. Watercolor painting provides a challenging activity for patients who are unable to do heavier work. Because any spilled paint washes out of linens, this medium can be taken to bed patients.

PROOFREADING

TABLE OF CONTENTS

	Page
PROOFREADER'S MARKS	1
Insert Period ... Caps-Used in Margin	1
Parentheses ... Lower Case-Used in Margin	2
Use Ligature ... Caps S Small Caps-Used in Text	3
TYPOGRAPHICAL ERRORS	4

PROOFREADING

PROOFREADER'S MARKS

⊙	INSERT PERIOD	▫	INDENT 1 EM
⋏	INSERT COMMA	▭	INDENT 2 EMS
⁏	INSERT COLON	¶	PARAGRAPH
?	INSERT QUESTION MARK	no ¶	NO PARAGRAPH
!	INSERT EXCLAMATION MARK	tr	TRANSPOSE-USED IN MARGIN
=/	INSERT HYPHEN	∽	TRANSPOSE-USED IN TEXT
⋎	INSERT APOSTROPHE	sp	SPELL OUT
⋎ ⋎	INSERT QUOTATION MARKS	ital	ITALIC-USED IN MARGIN
⊹	INSERT 1-EN DASH	――	ITALIC-USED IN TEXT
⊥	INSERT 1-EM DASH	b.f.	BOLDFACE-USED IN MARGIN
#	Insert Space	∿∿∿	BOLDFACE-USED IN TEXT
ld>	INSERT LEAD	s.c.	SMALL CAPS-USED IN MARGIN
shill	INSERT VIRGULE	═	SMALL CAPS-USED IN TEXT
⋁	SUPERIOR	rom.	ROMAN TYPE
⋀	INFERIOR	Caps.	CAPS-USED IN MARGIN

(/)	PARENTHESES	=	CAPS-USED IN TEXT
[/]	BRACKETS	l.c.	LOWER CASE-USED IN MARGIN
/	LOWER CASE-USED IN TEXT		
w.f.	LOWER CASE-USED IN TEXT		
⌢	CLOSE UP		
ℐ	DELETE		
ℐ̄	CLOSE UP AND DELETE		
℈	CORRECT THE POSITION		
⌐	MOVE RIGHT		
⌐	MOVE LEFT		
⊓	MOVE UP		
⊔	MOVE DOWN		
‖	ALIGN VERTICALLY		
=	ALIGN HORIZONTALLY		
⊐⊏	CENTER HORIZONTALLY		
⊔⊓	CENTER VERTICALLY		
⌣	PUSH DOWN SPACE		

⌒ USE LIGATURE

eq.# EQUALIZE SPACE-USED IN MARGIN

✓↲✓ EQUALIZE SPACE-USED IN TEXT

✓ DECREASE SPACE

stet LET IT STAND-USED IN MARGIN

······· LET IT STAND-USED IN TEXT

ⓧ DIRTY OR BROKEN LETTER

run over CARRY OVER TO NEXT LINE

runback CARRY BACK TO PRECEDING LINE

copy out SOMETHING OMITTED-SEE COPY

Au? ? QUESTION TO AUTHOR

∧ CARET-GENERAL INDICATOR USED TO MARK EXACT POSITION OF ERROR IN TEXT

⁏ INSERT SEMICOLON

C·oc CAPS & SMALL CAPS-USED IN MARGIN

≡ CAPS S SMALL CAPS-USED IN TEXT

TYPOGRAPHICAL ERRORS

It does not appear that the earliest printers had any method of correcting errors before the form-was on the press. The learned The learned correctors of the first two centuries of printing were not proofreaders in our sense; they were rather what we should term office editors. Their labors were chiefly to see that the proof corresponded to the copy, but that the printed page was correct in its Latinity; that the words were there, and that the sense was right. They cared but little about orthography, bad letters, or purely printers' errors, and when the text seemed to them wrong they consulted fresh authorities or altered it on their own responsibility. Good proofs, in the modern sense, were impossible until professional readers were employed — men who had first a printer's education, and then spent many years in the correction of proof. The orthography of English, which for the past century has undergone little change, was very fluctuating until after the publication of Johnson's Dictionary, and capitals, which have been used with considerable regularity for the past 80 years, were previously used on the miss-or-hit plan. The approach to regularity, so far as we have may be attributed to the growth of a class of professional proofreaders, and it is to them that we owe the correctness of modern printing. More errors have been found in the Bible than in any other one work. For many generations it was frequently the case that Bibles were brought out stealthily, from fear of governmental interference. They were frequently printed from imperfect texts, and were often modified to meet the views of those who published them. The story is related that a certain woman in Germany, who was the wife of a printer and lc./who had become disgusted with the continual assertions of the superiority of man over woman which she had heard, hurried into the composing room while her husband was at supper and altered a sentence in the Bible, which he was printing, so that it read Narr instead of Herr, thus making the verse read "And he shall be thy fool" instead of "And he shall be thy lord." The word not was omitted by Barker, the King's printer in England in 1632, in printing the seventh commandment. He was fined £3,000 on this account.

Glossary
OF TYPOGRAPHIC TERMS

A.A., A.C.—Abbreviation of Author's Alterations, Author's Corrections.

Accents—Marks over, under or through particular letters to show difference in pronunciation. For most roman and italic body letters, accents are cast on the letter. Separate accents are made for use with large or heavy-face types.

Advertising Rule – A thin brass rule, type-high and of varying thickness, used for dividing one advertisement from another on the printed page.

Agate—A small size of body type, corresponding to 5½ points, chiefly used now in classified advertising and market reports.

Agate Line—A standard of measurement for depth of columns of advertising space. Fourteen agate lines make one column-inch.

Alignment—An imaginary line at top or bottom of letters and characters.

Antique Type—A style of type in which all parts of the letters are of a uniform thickness of line, such as Bookman.

Arabic Figures—The characters 1, 2, 3, 4, etc. as distinguished from the Roman I, II, III, IV.

Ascending Letters – Those letters, like A, b, d, h, that occupy the upper two-thirds of the type body. The rising strokes of such letters are called *ascenders*.

Asterisk (or Star*)—One of the old-style reference marks. Also used to indicate omitted letters or words.

ATF – An abbreviation for American Type Founders, Elizabeth, N. J.

Author's Alterations—Changes required by the author (or buyer) after type has been correctly set to original specifications. Also called Author's Corrections.

Author's Proof—A clean proof sent to the author after the compositor's errors have been corrected.

Bad Break—Incorrect word-division.

Bastard Title—Short title preceding title page. On right-hand page, containing title of book only.

Bastard Type—(1) Type having a face larger or smaller than the size proper to the body, as 8-point face on a 9-point body, or 9-point face on a 8-point body. (2) Type not on the typographical point system.

Batter—Type injured in a type form.

Beard—Beveled space below the printing surface of a type letter.

Bearers – Strips of metal, type high, placed around jobs and pages that are to be electrotyped. Also used around type forms in reproduction proving, to insure even impression of paper on inked type.

BF.—Abbreviation for bold-face type.

Black Letter—Applied to many variations of a style of letter used in the early days of printing. Bibliographers call it gothic, because it has always been preferred by people of Gothic descent; but the style called Gothic among American printers is an entirely different letter.

Bodoni Dash – A tapered dash, thicker in the center than on the ends.

Body—The dimension of type from top to bottom of the letter; the thickness, or width sideways, is its "set width."

Body Type – Type used for straight composition in paragraphs or pages of one face; text letter.

Bold-Face—A name given to type that is heavier in face than the text with which it is used.

Border – A plain or ornamental frame around type composition.

Boxed, or Boxed-in—Small paragraphs or lines of type enclosed with rules or borders; paneled.

Box Head—A column heading in a ruled table; any heading enclosed in rules.

Brass Type—For stamping book covers, etc. Ordinary type metal cannot endure the heat which must be applied for stamping gold leaf, or printing on hard, rough surfaces. Brass types are more expensive as well as more durable.

Break – The place for ending or dividing a line of type.

Break-Up—To kill or to break up a form so that it cannot be printed again; metal will be consigned to the hellbox.

Break-Up for Color – An editorial instruction to divide a type form that is to be printed in more than one color, into separate forms for each of the colors.

Butted Slugs—A term used to describe matter which is too wide to set in one line on a composing machine. The matter is set on two slugs, these being placed end to end, or butted together to form one continuous line of type.

Calligraphic Type – Type design based upon styles of handwriting rather than upon the drawn letter.

Cap—An abbreviation of capital.

Caps, and Small Caps—Two sizes of capitals made on one size of type body, common in most roman fonts, and often set in combination: THIS IS CAPS AND SMALL CAPS.

Caption – A heading or explanation adjacent to a cut or picture.

Caret—A mark used in writing, proofreading, etc., to denote where a word or other matter is to be inserted.

Case – A receptacle for the storage of type or other composing materials. It is partitioned to keep the contents separated.

Casting Off—Estimating the amount of space a manuscript will occupy when set in type.

Cedilla—A mark under the letter c to indicate its pronunciation like s (ç).

Ceriphs, Cerifs, Serifs—Lines or cross strokes at the ends of the stem of a letter.

Chapter Heads—Those at the beginning of a chapter, usually sunk from the top line of a full page. The heads on second and succeeding pages are called running heads.

Character—Any single unit of type: a letter of the alphabet, a numerical digit, punctuation mark, a space between words, etc.

Circumflex – The caret-shaped accent placed over a letter, such as ô.

Clean Proof—A printer's proof containing few or no typographical errors.

Close Spacing – Thin spacing between words.

Close Up—In composition, to push type together and remove spacing leads.

Column Rule – A printing rule used to separate columns of type.

Composing Stick—A hand tool used by compositors to assemble type into lines. It is adjustable to different pica measures. The composing stick derived its name from the fact that the first ones were made from sticks of wood.

Composition – That part of printing which pertains to typesetting, making up, etc. Arranging the pages in a chase and locking up for the press is imposition.

Compositor—One who sets type; according to the class of work done, he is termed a book, newspaper, ad, or job compositor.

Compound Words—Two or more words connected with a hyphen, like merry-go-round.

Condensed—The word is applied commonly in printing to designate a type face thinner than normal, usually connected with the words which name it specifically. This face is normal.

Copper Spaces—Thin pieces of copper used in spacing and justifying lines of type. For easy identification, spaces of one-half-point thickness are copper, and one-point are brass.

Copy—The hand-written, typewritten or printed words or design given to the typographer. The term copy is also applied to a single specimen of a finished work.

Copy-Holder—One who holds copy and reads it aloud to the proofreader. Also, an arrangement placed on the compositor's case to hold copy while setting type.

Correcting—Changing wrong words, letters, types, etc., or adding new matter in type that has been set.

Cursive—Flowing italic form of type—imitation handwriting.

Cut-In Head—A heading set into a paragraph, either entirely or partly.

Cutoff Rule – A printing rule used to separate advertisements, and to separate different news items.

Dagger †, Double Dagger ‡—Reference marks.

Dashes—A mark of punctuation used to indicate an abrupt change in a statement, to connect side heads with their text, or in place of a colon to indicate that something is to follow.

Dead Matter—Type that has been used and is ready for distribution.

Deck Head – A heading having two or more groups of type.

Delete – A proofreader's mark used in correcting proof to show that designated letters, words, or sentences are to be omitted.

Descending Letters—Those letters, like p, y, j, g, q, that occupy the lower portion of the type body. The downward strokes of such letters are called *descenders*.

Diaeresis – Two dots placed over the second of two adjacent vowels to denote that they are to be pronounced separately.

Didot—European printers' unit of measurement – didot point .0148" – didot pica .1776".

Diphthong—Two vowels joined together; chiefly in words from the Latin. Modern usage often discards them.

Dirty Proof – A proof containing many typographical errors.

Display – Type composition in which various sizes and faces are used, like advertisements, title-pages, catalogs, etc., in distinction from straightaway work, which is composition in one size and one face, in uniform lines and paragraph form.

Display Type—A general term for those styles of type-faces designed for headings and advertisements, as distinguished from those used for plain reading matter.

Distribution—To put types back in their respective cases and boxes after use. In presswork, the uniform spreading of ink on rollers and face of the printing form.

Division of Words—The separation of words on syllables at the ends of lines; a necessary custom in type composition, in order to make lines of equal length and to avoid as much as possible unequal spacing between words.

Dot Leaders—Those cast with dots thus .... in distinction from hyphen leaders - - - - - - - -.

Drive Out – To space words widely to fill the line and drive out a word or syllable to the next line.

Drop-Folio—A page number placed at the bottom of a page.

Dummy – The preliminary drawing or layout showing the position of illustrations and text as they are to appear in the final reproduction.

Dump—A special table for assembling and correcting galleys. The word is also used synonymously with "kill," as a verb.

Dupe—A duplicate proof.

Em—The square of a type body. The common method of measuring type composition is by ems, the number of ems in a line being multiplied by the number of lines. The term is applied in many ways to printing material as em-dash—, em-quad.

Em Dash—A dash (—) one em long.

En—A unit of measure half as wide as an em of the same type.

Engraving—The act or art of producing letters or designs on wood, metal or other substances by cutting or corrosion, for the purpose of being printed on paper or other material.

Errata—Applied to a list of errors and corrections in a book which are of sufficient importance to be called to the attention of the reader; sometimes inserted at the beginning; or printed on a slip and tipped in beside the page containing the error.

Extended, Expanded – An extra wide face of type.

Extra Condensed—Used to describe a type face which has been compressed very thin sideways.

Face (of a type or form)—That part which prints, as distinguished from the shank and shoulder; also used to express one style of type from another, as plain face, heavy face, etc.

Feet—The bottom of the type body.

Floret – A small flower or part of a flower; in printing, the name is given to any flower or leaf-shaped type ornament.

Flush Paragraph – A paragraph having no indentation.

Folio – The number of a page.

Follow Copy – An instruction to the printer to set the type exactly like the copy in every detail.

Font – A complete assortment of type of one size and face.

Form – A page or number of pages, engravings or lines of type ready for printing.

Format – The size, form, proportions, etc., of a book or other work.

Furniture – In printing-office speech this term is given to all pieces of wood and metal designed to fill blank spaces between pages and around type-forms when locked in a chase. It is made in many lengths and widths.

Galley – The shallow tray used by compositors to hold type after the lines have been set.

Galley Proofs – Proofs pulled from type standing in a galley before being made up into pages.

Galley Rack – One in which already-composed galleys are kept.

Gothic – Type founders and printers in this country use this word to describe a style of type face of the plainest and simplest form, having no serifs or other useless strokes, and with lines of unvarying thickness. English printers call this style of type sans serif.

Guards or Guard-Lines – Strips of metal, type-high or a little higher, placed around type forms which are to be molded for electrotyping; sometimes called bearers.

Gutter – The blank space between columns of type.

Hairline – Used to describe any very fine or delicate line in type, brass rule or engraving; commonly applied to any character which is very light throughout.

Hair Spaces – Very thin spaces. Greatly facilitate the work of letter-spacing and justifying.

Halftone – An engraving plate made by photographic and chemical methods, in which the surface or printing part is composed of a series of light and heavy dots.

Hand Composition – The setting of type manually from a case with the use of a composing stick. Also, in a broader sense, to mean any hand work performed in a composing room.

Hand Proofs – Roughs pulled on a stone or manually operated proof press.

Hanging Figures – The so-called old-style figures (1, 2, 3, 4, 5, 6, 7, 8, 9).

Hanging Indention – That form of paragraph which is set with the first line full length and subsequent lines indented, as in these pages; usually employed in dictionaries, catalogs, price lists, etc.

Head – A display line at the top of an ad or other printed matter. The top of a page or book.

Head-Piece – The ornamental panel or picture placed at the top of a page in a book, usually at the beginning of chapters, where the open space left by the sinking of the heading is utilized for decoration.

Height-to-Paper – The measurement of type height from printing surface to bottom, including feet and face. This is not measured by points, but by thousandths of an inch.

Hellbox – A box containing old, damaged, or otherwise discarded type.

High Spaces, Quads and Leads – Used in type composition when the page is to be electrotyped.

Horsing – A newspaper proofroom term meaning to read a proof without copy.

Impose – To arrange pages in a chase so that they will appear in consecutive order when the printed sheets are folded.

Impression – The pressure given by a form of type or a plate to the sheet of paper.

Indent – To put a blank before or after words in a line, as at the beginning of a paragraph.

Indention or Indentation – Common paragraph indention is to begin the first line farther in from the margin than the other lines.

Inferior Letters or Figures—Undersized characters cast on the bottom of the type line for footnote references.

Initial—A large letter used at the beginning of important sections of a book or other printed matter.

Inline—A letter with white line cut in it.

Inverted Pyramid Head—
A heading in which the first line
is set to the full measure and
the others are increas-
ingly indented as
they are com-
posed, as
here.

Italic—The style of letters that slope forward, in distinction from upright, or roman, letters. Used for words requiring emphasis, extracts, bits of poetry, sub-headings, etc., and sometimes for prefaces and introductory paragraphs. Its use in roman text for names of books, plays, vessels, newspapers, etc., and for words from foreign languages, in common. A single line drawn under a word of sentence in written copy is a direction to the compositor to use italic.

Job Stick — A composing stick used on job work.

Jump Head — A headline over a news story that has been continued from another page.

Justify—To make lines of type the same length as their mates. This may be done by spacing between or within words, or at the ends of lines. To space a line is to put proper spaces between words or letters. A line may be well justified, but badly spaced, and vice versa.

Keep Standing—To hold composed type for further printing.

Kerned Letters—Those which have a part of the face projecting over the body of the type, like the italic f, j, K, V, W, etc.

Keyboard — That part of a typesetting machine that controls the flow of matrices in the composition.

Key Lines—Outline drawing on finished art containing only guide lines or those necessary for separation of colors on printing plates.

Key Plate — In color printing the key plate is the one used as a guide for obtaining the register of the other colors.

Kill—Take it out, throw it away, don't use. The accepted designation on all papers that either copy or type is to be discarded. To discard composed type matter after it is no longer of value.

Laying Type—Putting a font of type into cases.

Lay of Case—The plan or scheme of arrangement of the letters and other types in the compositor's case of hand type.

Layout Man — The duty of the layout man in the composing room is to prepare a rough diagram of a job that is to be set in type, and indicate the sizes and kinds of type that are to be used.

Leaders—Short dashes or dots placed at intervals in open lines to guide the eye across to figures or words at the ends, as in indexes, tables of contents, price lists, etc. They are cast in several styles such as fine dots, two dots to an em, one dot to an em. Used in commercial, legal and other forms where blank spaces are to be filled in by writing after the work is printed (the .... day of .... 19....).

Leads or Leds—Thin strips of soft metal used between lines of type to open them out more or less. They are made in different thicknesses, based on the point system.

Legend—The line or words under a cut briefly describing it.

LF—Abbreviation for light-face type.

Ligature — Two or more connected or tied letters cast on one body as œ, ff, fi, ffl and the capitals Æ and Œ.

Line Engraving—That style of engraving in which the effect is produced by lines or combinations of lines, in distinction from halftone and similar work in which the effects are obtained by masses of dots of larger or smaller dimensions.

Line Gauge—A strip of strong cardboard, wood or steel, having its edges marked with scales indicating ems of type sizes.

Lining Figures — Figures, usually of modern cut, that are cast so that they line together at the bottom, like 1 2 3 4 5 6 7 8 9 0, in distinction from the old-style figures: 1 2 3 4 5 6 7 8 9 0.

Linotype—A machine for setting type and casting it in lines instead of single characters.

Live Matter—Type composition or pages that have not yet been printed. After there is no further need of it, it is dead matter, ready for break up and distribution.

Locking Up – Tightening a form by means of quoins or screws, to prepare it for printing on the press.

Logotype – A complete item or word, cast on one body, such as a trademark.

Loose Justification – Term applied to lines in a stick when they are not properly spaced.

Machine Composition—Term applied to composition done on any typesetting or slugcasting machine.

Magazine—Where matrices are held in a composing machine.

Makeup—The arrangement of lines of type and illustrations into pages of proper length, with page numbers, heads, running heads, etc. This operation takes place after type in galley proofs has been corrected, and is just prior to the locking-up-for-printing process.

Making Ready—Preparing a form on the press for printing, by giving each part the proper impression, setting the gauges, etc. Comprises all the operations needed to make a satisfactory impression from a form.

Manuscript – Understood to include typewritten as well as handwritten words. Abbreviations, MS., plural, MSS.

Masthead—The name of a magazine or newspaper set in a distinctive type, or hand-lettered.

Matrice (or Matrix)—The shallow mold in which the face of a type is cast.

Measure—The width of a unit, column or page of type.

Misprint—A typographical error, made either through oversight or accident.

Mitre – A bevel on the ends of rules, so that they may join at an angle on corners.

Modern Roman—That general style of roman type face which is distinguished from the old-style roman by greater regularity of shapes, more precise curves and delicate hairlines and serifs.

Monotype Caster—A machine for automatically casting type in single characters.

Mortise – An opening made inside a printing plate to admit the insertion of type or other matter. If an area is cut away around the outside edge of a plate for type matter insertion it is called a "notch."

Movable Types – Characters or letters which are cast as individual types.

Nick – Shallow slit in a type which helps the compositor to avoid mixing with similar types.

Nonpareil—In the printer's measure it is half a pica, or approximately one-twelfth of an inch.

Numerals—The Arabic and Roman characters used to express numbers: 1, 2, 3, 4, 5, 6, 7, 8, 9, 0, or I, V, X, L, C, D, M, or i, v, x, l, c, d, m.

Office Corrections – Proofreader's changes made after the type has been set according to copy and for which the printer is responsible.

Office Style—The editorial style that is adopted by a printing office for the guidance of its compositors and proofreaders.

Off Its Feet—Type must stand squarely upright in order to give a good impression; when it leans one way or the other it is off its feet.

Offset—In letterpress printing, a smudge or an unwanted transfer of undried ink from a freshly printed sheet upon another sheet. Also the common expression for the lithographic printing process.

O. K. Proof—Mark of approval on proof.

O. K. with Changes (or corrections)—Mark of approval on proof, with minor changes.

Old English – The name given to a Church-like style of black-letter.

Old-Style – Old-Style and modern are the two general classes into which roman typefaces are divided; numberless varieties of both styles are made, and many of them are often difficult to place in one class or the other. In general, the true old-style in use today may be said to follow closely that of the Caslon form.

Old-Style Figures—see **Hanging Figures**.

Open Face Type—A type face in which the character prints in outline instead of as a solidly black letter; also called outline.

Open Spacing—Wide spacing, as in matter that is widely leaded.

Ornament—A floret or small decoration cast in type.

Out—A word or more omitted by mistake in composing.

Out of Sorts—To lack some of the necessary types in a case.

Out—See Copy—Marked on the margin of a proof to signify that the compositor has omitted something and directing him to refer to the copy.

Overhang — Anything that projects beyond the main body or slug is said to overhang.

Over-Run—To take words backward or forward from one line to another in correcting type.

Overset — Type set in excess of space needs in publications.

Page Proof—An impression of the type after it has been made up into page form.

Paragraph Mark — The most common form is this, ¶, which is really the letter P reversed, with the white part black and the black part white for distinctiveness.

Perforating Rule — Sharp, dotted rule slightly higher than type; it is placed in a form and perforates lines in a sheet to permit easy tearing off where desired, as in check books, coupon books, etc.

Pi—Types of different kinds mixed up in confusion.

Pica—Old name for a size of type equal to 12-point. It is the standard of measurement for leads, rules, furniture, and also for width and length of pages. Six picas equal, approximately, a linear inch.

Piece Fractions—Fractions made up of two or more types; the numerator and denominator cast separately, usually on bodies half the size of the whole numbers of the type with which they are used. Sometimes called split fractions.

Pig — A bar of type-metal, molded in convenient form, to replenish metal pots in type-casting and slug-casting machines.

Pi-ing—The act of mixing type in confusion; accidentally pushing words or lines of type apart so that they fall off their feet and become scattered.

Plain Rule — Printing rule with plain, straight lines, as distinguished from dotted and ornamental rule.

Point Size — The dimension of a type from the back to the front of the base; sometimes called body size.

Point System—The sizes of type cast by type founders are graduated on a uniform scale known as the point system. The unit of the system is a division of space called a point (.0138 of an inch), and all type bodies are multiples of and are measured by it. Each size is described by its number of points. Calculations are simplified ordinarily by assuming the point as one-seventy-second of an inch.

Poster Type—Large sizes for billboard printing, mostly made of wood.

Press Proof—Proofs of type and engravings made on a printing press before the start of the press run.

Progressive Proofs — The impressions taken singly from each of the color-plates of a set, showing each color alone, and in proper color combination and rotation with each succeeding color to display the final printed result.

Proof—A trial impression taken from a printing surface.

Proofreading—The procedure involving detailed checking of any typeset matter against manuscript for the purpose of eliminating errors or imperfections before final proofing or printing.

Quads — Metal blanks used for large spaces in composing type.

Quoins — (Pronounced Coins) — Steel, wedge-shaped devices, usually triangular, and less than type-high, used to lock type and plates rigidly in chases for the press.

Raised Initial—An initial which projects upward from the first line of type; sometimes called stick-up initial.

Record—A monotype machine's paper roll, which keyboard operation perforates and which, subsequently, regulates type casting.

Recto—Right hand side, odd-numbered pages in a book.

Register—To adjust the pages of a form so that they will print exactly on the back of those printed on the first side; to impose a form or to fix the gauges on the press so that the pages when printed back to back on the sheet, will be in the proper places. To print two or more colors, beside each other, or one over the other, so that they will print in the proper places.

Reglets—Thin strips of wood similar to leads, 6-point and thicker, used as substitute for leads and slugs in line spacing.

Reproduction Proof — A perfect printed impression of type and/or engravings for purposes of photographic reproduction.

Reversal Plate—An engraving, when the object facing left is made to face right, or vice versa. Achieved by flopping negative.

Revise—A proof taken after corrections have been made; to compare a proof so taken with the one on which errors are marked, to see if corrections are properly made.

Rivers — Spaces between words, accidentally coinciding in successive lines and forming "rivers" of white in the type mass.

Roman Figures—Numerals expressed by letters as disinguished from those expressed by Arabic characters: as I, II, III, etc.

Roman Type—The common form of letter face, such as is used for the text of this book; it is the kind of letter preferred for books and newspapers by English-speaking people and by the Latin races. Roman letter is distinguished from italic, with which it is often mated; from Greek, with which it has many characters in common; and from black letter or Old English, as well as from script or handwriting, etc.

Rough — Preliminary visualization of a drawing.

Rough Proof — A proof taken without special care.

Rule—Thin strips of type metal, type-high and varying in thickness, from 1-point to 24-point, for printing straight lines and borders.

Run-Around — The term describing a type area set in measures that are adjusted to fit around a picture or another element of the design.

Run-In — Combining one or more sentences in order to avoid making an additional paragraph.

Run-In Cut—A cut set into the page in such a way that there is type-matter on three sides of it.

Running-Head or Running-Title — The title of a book or subject placed at the top of each page of a book.

Sans Serif Type Family—This family of letter, which is characterized by the absence of serifs and the construction of the letters from strokes of equal thickness, based on a regular form of the oldest Roman inscriptional letters. No Sans Serif types were known before 1816.

Scotch Rule—One combining a light and a heavy line.

Script—A general name for the class of types designed to imitate handwriting.

Serif—The short cross-line or trick at the end of the main strokes in roman letters.

Set Close—To thin space and omit leads.

Set Open—To wide space and open out well with leads and slugs.

Set Solid—To set lines of type close together, without leads or other material.

Setwise — A term used to differentiate the width of a type from its body size.

Shoulder—The blank space on the top of a type not covered by the letter; specifically, the space above and below the letter.

Sidehead—A flush heading set to one side of the type page or column, also called a side note. A heading cut into the outer margin of text, either wholly or partially, is often termed a "Cut-In Side Head."

Slip Sheet—To prevent freshly printed sheets from smudging with ink as they come off the press, a piece of paper is placed or slipped between the sheets.

Slug—A strip of metal, usually 6 points thick, used for spacing. A line of type cast on a Linotype, Intertype or Ludlow Machine.

Slur — A blurred image of the form being reproduced, due to movement, during impression, of the sheet of paper being printed.

Small Capitals — Capital letters which are approximately the size of the lower case characters of the font, used frequently for subheadings, running titles, etc.

Solid Matter — Lines of type set close together without leads.

Sorts — The letters in the boxes of a case or any particular letters or characters of a font, in distinction from the complete assortment. "Out of sorts," short of particular letters; "runs on sorts," when the copy calls for more than the usual number of any letters.

Space Out — To insert spaces between words or letters in order to make the line of type cover a specified measure.

Spaces — Thin metal blanks used to separate words in a line.

Spacing — The insertion of spaces, leads, or slugs to separate and justify words, lines, or paragraphs.

Specimen Page — A sample page; it may be of a proposed book or to show the use of certain types, borders, etc. In all important work a specimen page is first set in order to approve the type, size, and other details.

Square Indentation — An arrangement of type matter in which all the lines of one paragraph are indented both left and right, within the margin of the other paragraphs; usually used for quotations, extracts, etc.

Squared Up — In speaking of type, squared up means the lines come even by changing space between words or adding space between letters. Squaring-up of forms means putting a trisquare around to test its squareness, and if not square, making it so.

Standard Spacing — The ideal, uniform space that should exist between words ending and beginning with ordinary rounded letters.

Standing Matter — Composed type which is kept set up from one printing to another to save resetting.

Steel Furniture — A modern improvement on printers' wood and soft metal furniture; its great advantage being durability, rigidity and usually lighter weight than ordinary metal.

Stem (of letter) — The main upright stroke of a letter.

Stet — Written opposite a word in proof, to signify that it is wrongly marked out and shall remain as is.

Stick — A composing stick.

Straight Matter — Plain composition, in ordinary paragraph form, as distinguished from display, or that set in special arrangement.

Strip Material — Leads, slugs, dashes, rules, column rules, borders, and the like, produced in long strips by special machines in the printing plant, and then cut or sawed to required lengths as needed.

Subhead — A secondary headline or title.

Sunken Initial — An initial sunken into an indention in the type lines, so that the upper edge of the initial is level, or nearly so, with the top of the first line of type.

Superior Letters or Figures — Undersized characters cast at the top of the type line, usually for footnote references.

Swash Letters — Italic capitals with little flourishes which fill up the gaps made by the inclination of the letters, etc. They are furnished as extra characters for several kinds of italic, and are best used in occasional places only.

Syllable — A part of a word, which may be spoken by one effort of the voice; it may be represented by one letter (a vowel) or by a number of letters. In typesetting, the division of words at the ends of lines is made between two syllables, never properly in the middle of a syllable.

Symmetry — Regular arrangement of parts across a given axis so that a division through that axis will give similar halves. A type design is said to be symmetrical when, after drawing a line through it from top to bottom, each type line is divided exactly in half, thus leaving equal type masses on both sides.

Tabular Work — Composition which involves columns of type, often with vertical and horizontal rules. Any matter so composed is called a table.

Text—The body matter of a page or of a book, as distinguished from titles, headings, notes, extracts, references, indexes and other auxiliary matter. The word text is also used to describe the Old English or black letter style of type, probably from the fact that the text of the first books was printed in black letter.

Three-Line Initial—An initial letter having a depth equal to three lines of text matter.

Two-Line Initial—An initial letter having the depth of two lines of text matter.

Tying Up—Using string binding to hold composed type pages together.

Type Face—A particular type design, usually designated by the name of the designer.

Type Family—The name given to two or more series of types which are variants of one design.

Type High—The height of type in America is .918 of an inch. Electros, engravings and other forms to be printed on a typographic press should conform to the type-high standard.

Type Series—The name given to the number of sizes of one design of type faces. Example: Cheltenham Oldstyle series has fourteen sizes.

Typewriter Type—Made to imitate the work of typewriting machines. Its peculiarity is that every character and space is the same width.

Typographia—Relating to typography and kindred subjects. This word has been used as a title for books relating to printing and as the name of a society of printers.

Typographical Error—Error resulting from a mistake of any variety in composing type matter.

Typographic Design—Design according to which type and related matter is laid out in form.

Uncials—A style of pen-written letters in early Latin manuscripts. They were a combination of the old capitals and the newer minuscule or small letters, in use before small letters had been developed into the easier-made forms which they finally assumed, and which are now familiar.

Upright Page—One that measures less sideways than it does up and down; the usual shape of a book page, as distinguished from the oblong page, which is wider than its height.

Verso—Left-hand side, even-numbered pages of a book or magazine.

Widow—A single word, in a line by itself, ending a paragraph. Widows are frowned upon in good typography.

Wood Type—Large types, such as are used for posters and billboards, are made of wood. The smallest size for practical use is 48-point, or 4-line pica. Sizes of wood type are multiples of the pica, and are so named, as 8-line, 10-line, etc.

Work-Ups—Unwanted impressions of spaces, quads or under type-high matter on a printed sheet.

Wrong Font—A wrong letter or character in a line, caused by mixing fonts of type; in proof, written wf.

X Height—The height of the main, or central, portion of lower case letters, exclusive of ascenders and descenders.